301

Bright
Ideas
for
Busy
Kids

11 Messy Projects, **12** Silly Games,
10 Cool Things to Make and
Hundreds of Other Ways
to Spend Time Creatively

Silvana Clark

SOURCEBOOKS, INC.®
NAPERVILLE, ILLINOIS

Published by Sourcebooks, Inc.
P.O. Box 4410, Naperville, Illinois 60567-4410
(630) 961-3900
FAX: (630) 961-2168
www.sourcebooks.com

Library of Congress Cataloging-in-Publication Data

Clark, Silvana
  301 bright ideas for busy kids : 11 messy projects, 12 silly games, 10 cool things to make and hundreds of other ways to spend time creatively
/ by Silvana Clark.
    p. cm.
  ISBN 1-4022-0050-1 (pbk. : alk. paper)
  1. Amusements. 2. Parent and child. I. Title: Three hundred and one bright ideas for busy kids. II. Title.
GV1203 .C54 2002
793—dc21

                        2002153442

Printed and bound in the United States of America
BG 10 9 8 7 6 5 4 3 2

Dedication

People always ask me how I come up with ideas for family activities. If they were to spend more than an hour with my husband, Allan, they'd see where my ideas originate. His fourth grade teacher was right when she wrote on his report card, "Allan is a fun-fun-fun boy."

Thanks, Allan, for being my best friend and helping us to be a fun-fun-fun family. Thanks also, Sondra, for being such a willing participant in trying out family activities. No matter what we do, it's always more fun when you are there with your dimples and wide smile. I love you both.

Acknowledgments

Although we live entirely different lives on different ends of the United States, my agent Linda Konner and I share a love for the publishing world. We each do our part. I simply write the books. She does the time-consuming, behind-the-scenes work. Without her hard efforts, I'd be writing manuscripts and storing them on my shelf. Thanks, Linda, for your help in getting my books on actual bookstore shelves.

Thanks also to my editor, Deb Werksman, who instinctively knew how I love to work. She told me what she wanted, then left me alone to get the job done. We three make a great team!

A special thanks goes to Jerry Chambers of Chambers Chevrolet in Bellingham, Washington. He played a pivotal role in getting our family the use of a Chevy truck so we could take a one-year trip around the United States. Hopefully, as Allan, Sondra, and I travel and present parenting workshops, we can inspire other families to experience the joy of having fun together. If we survive being together for twelve months in a travel trailer, we might even have enough material for another book!

Introduction

In the rush of daily life, we parents get so involved in supervising bedtime routines or checking homework that we often forget to have fun with our children. For ten years, I was recreation supervisor for the local parks and recreation department. Every week, I'd observe families actively involved in fun events. I saw parents and children laughing together, and a sense of closeness generated among family members. That's what having fun does to families: it strengthens the family unit and creates the kinds of memories that last a lifetime.

Enjoying family time together truly is important, and it's not so difficult to make it happen. As the adult, you'll be the one planning the activities, but you'll be encouraged by the positive feedback you get from your kids, and you'll find yourself having more fun than you've had since you were, well, a kid.

301 Bright Ideas for Busy Kids provides a wide variety of ideas for enjoyable time with your children. With everyone's busy schedules, sometimes all there's time for is a ten-minute game after dinner; but it sets a positive tone for the entire evening.

Most of the entries in *Bright Ideas* require supplies you're likely to have at hand already. All the activities are designed to provide maximum fun with minimum preparation, and are easily adaptable to fit your family. If you have no interest in cooking or baking, try building a tooth fairy hotel or organizing a spontaneous neighborhood bike parade. Whether it's mixing up a batch of mystery slime at the kitchen table, playing water balloon volleyball in the backyard, or holding a tall tales picture contest on a car trip, these ideas will generate laughter and positive memories.

So whether it's sunny or rainy, grab an idea, grab your children, and prepare to have fun!

Family
Fun

1. Secret Family Pals

Supplies: paper, pencils, empty bag

Many offices conduct a "Secret Pal" program during the holidays. Turn this activity into a year-round family event.

Write everyone's name on a piece of paper. Put the slips into a bag and randomly draw names so that no one gets their own name. Keep the identities secret! Each family member now has a secret pal.

Set a time limit, such as five or ten days, during which everyone does a daily secret good act for his or her pal. Part of the fun is guessing who is making your bed or writing you nice notes. Some things you can do for your secret pal are:

- ☺ Add a special treat to their lunch sack.
- ☺ Make a card and stick it in their pocket.
- ☺ Buy their favorite dessert.
- ☺ Give a coupon for a special treat (redeemable after secret pals are identified).
- ☺ Set a bunch of flowers by their dinner plate.
- ☺ Write a poem about their positive traits.
- ☺ Secretly do one of their chores.

This activity requires family members to think about others. It's also fun to wake up and find a small gift next to your bowl of cereal!

2. Growing Family Tree

Supplies: large piece of butcher paper or bulletin-board paper from a school-supply a store, markers, photographs, scissors, glue

Children have a natural curiosity about their relatives. "Does Grandma have a mom and dad?" "Do we have any famous historical people in our background?" "What does it mean that Sam is my second cousin, once removed?" Instead of plotting your family tree on a single sheet of paper, use a life-sized "tree."

Get a large piece of blank newsprint or butcher paper. Many school-supply stores sell colored paper by the yard, so you don't have to buy a huge fifty-foot roll.

Place the paper on a hard surface so it is easy to write on. To help children understand the concept of a family tree, find an example for them to study. It's sometimes difficult to understand who is related to whom and just how to diagram that relationship.

Begin your family tree with the most important people: your children. Have them draw their pictures at the top of the paper. From there, move down and list or draw immediate family members. For even more clarity, use a different color marker for each side of the family. If you are extra-ambitious, glue photos of family members onto the family tree. This process results in many funny stories like, "Remember when Grandma played touch football with us and then tackled the referee?"

At some point you'll need to start making calls, asking relatives, "Do you know the name of great-great Uncle Elmer's cousin?" Even if you can't trace your history back to Adam and Eve, your children will get a clearer picture of how they are part of a long history of interrelated people. Hang your super-sized family tree in a prominent location. At holiday gatherings, people will add information and even more amusing anecdotes about family members.

3. Fancy Family Flags

Supplies: rip-stop nylon fabric, fabric glue, scissors, wooden dowels

If the queen of England gets a flag, why shouldn't each of your family members have one also? With a few simple items, you can create a distinct flag to display on birthdays or special events.

Make a family trip to the fabric store. Let each family member select a half-yard of his or her favorite color of rip-stop nylon. It's available in a number of bright colors. The nylon lets you display the flag outdoors in all kinds of weather. Also buy a few quarter-yard strips of other assorted colors.

When you get home, cut the half-yard sections into pieces about 12" x 18". Lay a dowel along one of the shorter edges and fold the fabric over it. Sew or glue the fabric to itself, forming a casing for the flag. Remove the dowel while you finish decorating the flag.

Let each family member decorate his or her flag. Using the remaining scraps of nylon, cut out shapes such as circles, flowers, or stars. Encourage children to decorate their flags according to their hobbies or interests. Attach the cutouts to the flag with fabric glue. Let the glue dry before waving the flags in the air. Slip a dowel back into the casing for your flagpole. When someone has a birthday or gets an *A* on their spelling test, display their flag for everyone to see. Make sure adults make a flag, also. That way, the next time you get a promotion, your flag will fly proudly in the front yard!

4. Pictorial Measure Chart

Supplies: 5- or 6-foot-long narrow piece of wood or tape measure, markers, photos, glue

It's a family ritual. Every six months or so, a child says, "Dad! I think I've grown. Measure me on the wall." An adult dutifully measures and makes a tiny pencil line on the wall, indicating another growth spurt...and the need for another pair of new shoes. Instead of registering your child's growth with chicken-scratch lines on a doorjamb, turn the event into a priceless timeline.

Glue a tape measure or simply paint a narrow board and attach it to the wall, marking inches like a giant yardstick. Here's where the "priceless timeline" comes in. As the children stand next to the marker, add a recent photo by the measurement. This gives a permanent record of their height and their cute little faces.

If your children are already older, add a few pictures of their younger (and shorter) years lower down on your measuring tool.

5. Family Collages

Supplies: old magazines, scissors, glue, 11" x 18"
construction paper or cardboard
optional: snacks

Most of us think of collages as those pieces of cardboard covered with globs of glue, sticks, and leaves made by enthusiastic preschoolers. When your children are older, try a more advanced version of the collage.

Set out an assortment of magazines, scissors, and glue. Give each person a sheet of 11" x 18" construction paper. Explain that artistic ability doesn't matter, since all you have to do is cut and paste. Have family members go through the magazines and cut out photographs, words, or phrases that describe them and their interests.

Have snacks handy and let the conversation flow as people say, "Anyone found a picture of a horse?" "Sarah, I found this headline that says 'Soccer.' Do you need it?" As people cut out pictures, glue them onto the construction paper, collage style, with overlapping edges. You can toss scraps in a big trash can as you go, but it's more fun to just disregard all the scraps of paper littering the floor.

After the collages are complete, collect all of them. One at a time, hold a collage up and see if the rest of the family can guess who made it. Then have the proud artist explain some of the pictures and what they represent. You'll gain new insight about each other, plus have a colorful reminder of your time together. For long-term use, get the collages laminated at a print shop and use them as personalized placemats.

6. My Busy Week

Supplies: camera, film, photo album, markers

Toddlers love looking at books illustrating everyday events such as taking a bath and playing with the dog. They especially enjoy photos of themselves doing ordinary things. Combine these two elements by periodically making a book titled "My Busy Week."

Don't worry if your child is older than a toddler. Begin the book soon, no matter the age of your child. You have ten to twelve years to complete your series of books! All you need is a camera and a small 4" x 6" photo album. Designate a few days to take pictures of your child on a regular basis. They'll probably complain as you snap them brushing their teeth, but just explain that you are like the paparazzi with a famous movie star.

Since the title of the book is "_____'s Busy Week," you want to document the ordinary experiences of their life. Photograph them eating, getting on the bus, playing soccer, etc. Try to sneak into their room and take a picture of your little angel fast asleep. If possible, show up at school for a few classroom pictures.

After the pictures are developed, place them in chronological order in the miniature photo album. Begin with breakfast, combing their hair, walking to school, etc. Label the album with the year. Approximately one year later, bring out the camera to begin another week-long photo documentary of your child's life. After the photo album is complete, bring out the previous year's book and compare the two. Children enjoy reliving their year and noticing, "Oh, look! Last year I played the piano and now I'm playing the clarinet." It's especially fun to look back over several years of your child's life as they reminisce with the photo albums.

7. Family Portraits

Supplies: paper, watercolors, markers or crayons,
two or more family members
Optional: easels, art instruction books

Your family may not be able to visit France to see the actual Mona Lisa, but you can still expose your children to the world of fine art. Simply set up an artist's gallery in the comfort of your own home. The talent displayed will surpass any Rembrandt or van Gogh.

Transform a room into an art gallery with a few avant-garde touches. Put a sign on the door saying "Galleria of Exquisite Art." Set out a variety of artistic supplies such as watercolors, markers, and good old crayons. If possible, borrow a few easels to complete the feel of a working gallery.

Assemble your family, otherwise known as the artists, in one room. Display and share a few books about drawing portraits. Don't worry about giving a full art lesson. Just share two or three tips you gathered by skimming the books.

Write everyone's name on a piece of paper and put them in a bag. Take turns reaching into the bag and selecting the name of a family member you will draw. If Emily draws Sarah's name, that means Emily situates herself so she can see Sarah. In the meantime, Sarah is sketching Mom, who is drawing Brandon. Encourage people to use a variety of mediums. Sketch the portrait with colored markers, and then fill in areas with watercolors. Make a border design with crayons.

After the drawing session, take turns admiring each other's work. Display the family faces in a prominent location.

8. Crazy Communication Centers

Supplies: manila envelopes or construction paper and stapler, markers, stickers, thumbtacks, two or more family members

Parents strive to create an atmosphere of open communication with their children. Yet somehow, children go through periods when their only conversation consists of "What?" or "I don't know." When verbal communication is lacking, try using these family communication centers.

Give every family member a plain manila envelope. If you don't have those, staple two pieces of construction paper together to form a homemade envelope. Spend some time decorating each envelope with markers or stickers to give them a personal touch. While you're decorating, explain the purpose of this activity.

Sometimes it's difficult to express what you want to say with words. These envelopes, placed on everyone's bedroom door, are for written notes. Maybe you're mad at a sibling. Write a note telling them how you feel. Perhaps a family member did something extra nice. Jot a few lines of appreciation and drop the note in their mail envelope.

Parents might need to get this activity going by writing positive notes to all the children. They'll see how fun it is to get "mail" and start writing on their own.

9. What Do You Really Do?

Supplies: paper, pencils, bag or box

You might be the CEO of a multi-billion-dollar company, but in your child's eyes you're only "Mom" or "Dad." Even if you hold a more traditional job such as a teacher or store manager, children have trouble seeing their parents in a "professional" light.

Try this easy activity to find out what your children really know about you and other family members. Begin by writing everyone's name on a piece of paper. Put the slips in a bag and draw names, keeping the results secret. Each person pantomimes one characteristic of the person they selected. Try to guess who it is. When your eight-year-old pantomimes talking on the phone, it won't be hard to guess he's depicting your teenager.

It's interesting to see how children view their parents' lives. One hard-working architect saw himself in a new light as his daughter pantomimed him sitting with a sketchpad drawing stick figures and eating cookies. After everyone has a turn, toss the names into the bag again to select new names. Do two or three rounds of pantomimes. Take time afterward to clear up any misconceptions!

10. Fantastic Family Traditions

Supplies: varies

Some families have elaborate traditions, such as creating handmade gifts for birthdays or writing extensive family histories for future generations. If simplicity is more your style, try some of these easy and meaningful family traditions:

- Designate one day each year for "Family Day." This is a day specifically for family fun, special foods, and being together. Pick a day between holidays when everyone needs a mental pick-up.
- Plan a special "date" with each of your children. Write it in your calendar and schedule other events around it. Let the child decide what to do. You might find yourself just sitting by the fireplace with hot chocolate and looking through photo albums with your daughter.
- Designate a giant "change" can or jar. Place loose change in the jar and use it for special family trips or treats. Soon children will contribute when they have a bit of extra money.
- Create silly traditions such as group hugs. When someone is upset, call out, "Sam needs a group hug." Some families have a secret gesture that means "I love you." When you're in a crowded room, glance at your son, rub your eyebrow and smile. He'll know you're conveying your love.
- One family has a yearly tradition of making a junk-food cake. A large sheet cake is stacked with donuts, cookies, Twinkies, and other sugar-laden treats. Each layer of "junk" is held in place with frosting!
- Traditions can be as simple as eating dinner together and sharing the best thing that happened during the day.

11. Year-Round Family Fun

Supplies: paper, pencil

Instead of moaning, "I really should spend more time with my family," plan a year's worth of activities ahead of time. It's not as hard as it sounds. Once the list is made, all you have to do is carry out the ideas.

On a day when you have some peace and quiet (does such a day exist?), come up with fifty-two family activities. If you need ideas, just look through this book! They don't have to be elaborate or expensive. You'll then give your children a packet with fifty-two slips of paper, each listing something to do.

Pick a day each week when a child selects one slip of paper. Then decide when during the week that event will take place. Perhaps the activity is, "Go out for ice cream sundaes," or, "Build a birdhouse together." Other ideas are:

Get $1.00 each to spend at the video arcade.
Play hide-and-seek as a family.
Stay up extra late on the weekend.
Pick out your favorite dessert from the deli.
Go on a bike ride.
Go bowling.

Children know that every week for an entire year, you'll do at least one fun thing together...and probably many more!

12. Family Time Capsule

Supplies: coffee can or box with lid, markers or paints, assorted memorabilia

For children, the idea of ten years from now seems like an eternity. For adults, it's a fleeting moment. Create a family time capsule by gathering precious items to store and view again in ten years.

Select a storage container. A large coffee can with a plastic lid or a purchased storage box works well. Let younger children be in charge of decorating the containers. Use permanent markers or paints to add color and individualize the time capsule.

Ask each family member to select three or four small items that have special meaning for him or her. As children place the items in the storage container, have them share why the item has significance. A child might put in a picture of a bike, because she just learned to ride a two-wheeler. Someone else might add a report card, showing their dedication to school. Include a copy of the day's newspaper. Seal the items inside.

As a family, decide where to store the time capsule. Some families simply stick it on a shelf in the garage. Others make a big production of digging a hole and actually burying the container. Set a date ten years from now when the family gathers and opens the container. The only hard part of this activity is remembering where you hid your time capsule!

13. Expand Your Horizons

Supplies: pencil, calendar

Most children will wholeheartedly try a new activity if it sounds like fun to them. Learn to ride a skateboard? Why not! Want to go up the rock-climbing wall? Sure, they'll do it. On the other hand, ask an adult to try something new and they don't want to get out of their comfort zone. Who, me? Join an aerobics class? No way!

This activity requires parents to participate and set a good example. (You always set a good example, don't you?) When the family is casually together, announce the new "Expand Your Horizons" program that is soon to begin. Assign every family member a specific week and write it on the calendar. During your assigned week, you must learn something new and share it with other family members. For example:

- Get a book on origami. Learn to make several paper sculptures and teach the family.
- Find a new recipe and try it out on the family.
- Teach the dog a new trick and share tips on dog training.
- Ask the neighbor to show you how she grows such large tomatoes. Give a mini-gardening lesson.
- Ask a dance teacher to show you some advanced steps. Practice with family members.
- Learn to set up a super-easy family website. Share the results.

Sharing knowledge is a wonderful way to gain self-confidence. With everyone participating, your family will gain new skills and an awareness of each person's capabilities. Even a kindergartner can show everyone the correct way to tie a shoe.

Family Fun

15

14. Bag of Magical Fun

Supplies: index cards, markers, bag

Your children's desire to spend time with you overshadows yearly trips to Disneyland. Often children are happy just helping Dad wax the car, as long as it allows for uninterrupted time together. Keep a supply of togetherness activities handy by making a magical fun bag.

Set out two piles of different-colored index cards. One color is for quick and easy activities, while the other color symbolizes something requiring more time and preparation. For the next week or so, encourage your children to jot down things they like doing as a family on the cards. Casually ask a few questions about their favorite pastimes and let them jot down answers. The point is to compile a list of games, crafts, and other activities as a resource list. Possible questions could be:

- ✿ What things do you like to do in the backyard?
- ✿ What are your favorite rainy day activities?
- ✿ What snacks can you make on your own with little adult supervision?
- ✿ What is your favorite place to go within a ten-minute drive from the house?
- ✿ What are your favorite board games?
- ✿ What kind of crafts do you like to make?
- ✿ What's your favorite music to listen to?
- ✿ What's your favorite activity to do with an adult?

By the time your children list answers to some of these questions, you should have an extensive resource list. Your children may come up with unique ideas:

- ● Tell me about the day I was born.
- ● Walk to the store with me for a treat.
- ● Help me clean my room.
- ● Dad, let me put Mom's makeup on you!

- Let's discuss giving me a raise in my allowance.
- Read to me while I take a bath.

Keep the cards in a special satin or velvet bag. Let your children know they can add ideas to the bag at any time. As often as possible, have children select a card from the magical bag and enjoy time together.

Another option is to set up file folders or a box with activities sorted into categories such as "Crafts," "Outdoor Fun," etc. Any time you happen to read a magazine article about family activities, you can drop it in a file. Maybe the local paper has a column on "Free Things to Do with the Kids." Cut it out for future reference. Soon you'll have a wonderful set of instant ideas the whole family can refer to when they're looking for something to do!

15. Swimsuit Sequence

Supplies: camera; item of adult clothing,
such as a swimsuit, shirt, or dress

We all know how quickly children grow up. Once they get through the colicky stage, children seem to jump from one developmental stage to another. Physically, they develop from chubby toddlers to lanky preteens.

Here's a unique way of documenting your child's growth beyond the measurement marks on your kitchen door. To get the full effect, you should start on their first birthday, but don't despair if your child is already six or seven years old. On your child's next birthday, have them put on a specific item of adult clothing, such as a shirt or dress. The clothes are not supposed to fit, so let them hang. Take a picture of your child. Then save that item of clothing for the following year. At your child's next birthday, have them put on the same shirt for another picture. Soon you'll end up with a chronological record of your child growing into what once was a baggy piece of clothing. One dad purchased a woman's swimsuit for his daughter's first birthday. He took a picture of the baby inside a huge suit. Twelve years later, he has twelve pictures of his daughter in the same swimsuit. (Everyone is impressed that he finds the suit year after year!)

If the clothing seems too complicated, take a chronological picture each year of your child standing in front of the same door or by the same tree. It's great to look at one page in a photo album and see many years of growth.

16. Family Concentration

Supplies: two or more people, camera, film, index cards, glue

If your family is like most, at one time or another you've played the popular game of Concentration. Young children can match pairs of six or eight cards. Older children, with their good memories, easily play with many more cards. Here's a way to play Concentration while incorporating your whole family.

Get a new roll of film and take pictures of your family in distinctive clothing or making goofy faces. Include the family pets also. Try to get at least twelve to fifteen pictures. When getting the film developed, ask for double prints. For durability, glue each photo on a plain index card. The photos are now your Concentration cards.

Mix the photos and lay them out on the table in even rows. The first player turns over two cards. He might see a picture of Dad sticking out his tongue and a picture of himself wearing a baseball hat. Since those cards don't match, he returns them to their original position and another player turns two cards over. As soon as two cards match, that player removes the cards and gets another turn. Continue playing until all the cards are gone and you are tired of looking at everyone's silly faces.

17. Early Morning Exploration

Supplies: none

Saturday morning. That wonderful feeling of being able to sleep in as late as you want without having to race off to school or work. Children slowly wake up and watch cartoons while eating their favorite cereal. While everyone needs to relax, pick one Saturday morning to break out of your weekend routine and go for an early morning exploration.

Explain to your children the night before that everyone will be waking up early to explore the neighborhood. Quiet their groans of displeasure by bribing them with doughnuts for breakfast.

Get the family up very early on Saturday and prepare to explore the neighborhood. If you live in a rural area, you might want to take a short drive to a nearby town or neighborhood. Some families explore on bikes. There's a whole new aspect to seeing the area where you live while walking or riding bikes early in the morning. It's usually quiet, with fewer cars than on a weekday. Show your children how twenty-four-hour-a-day businesses serve customers even in the wee hours of daylight. Wave to passing joggers. Watch vendors set up at a local farmers' market. Don't forget to have fresh-baked doughnuts for breakfast.

18. Rainy Day Exploration

Supplies: rain and mud

Parents are very predictable. We tell our children not to jump on furniture, we insist on bicycle helmets, and we try to provide semi-healthy foods. Children know exactly what we'll say or do. Throw your children for a loop by doing something totally unpredictable. The next time it rains, run through the house yelling, "Everyone get boots and raincoats and meet me at the front door in two minutes!" You'll have children rushing to find long-lost boots and wondering if dear old mom and dad have finally lost their senses.

As everyone gathers by the front door, change your demeanor and act as if this is an everyday occurrence. Calmly state, "Since it's 7:00 P.M. and raining, I think this is the perfect time for a delightful walk in the rain. Please follow me and be sure to jump in lots of mud puddles." Can you imagine the look on your child's face? Being open to new experiences, they'll willingly take a rain walk. Try these activities:

◆ Take turns jumping over mud puddles. A running start helps them get over the huge puddles. If you can't make it over the puddle...that's what boots are for.
◆ Reenact the popular musical *Singing in the Rain*. Link arms, pick a song, and walk down the street singing like Broadway chorus line singers.
◆ Help clear away any debris caught in street drains by the sidewalk. It's fun watching the dammed-up water gush toward the drain.
◆ Wave to people inside their dry homes. They'll wonder what you are up to.
◆ When you get home, sit around with cups of hot chocolate and listen to your children tell you what a great parent you are.

19. Grocery Store Games

Supplies: grocery store, coupons

Watch adults in a grocery store. Their goal is to get in, load up the groceries, and get out as soon as possible. For children, an ordinary grocery store is filled with interesting sights and smells. Of course, it's also filled with candy!

Instead of racing through the store, take time to explore with your children. Try these ideas:

☺ Head toward the spice aisle and ask the children to look at the price-per-pound labels. They'll be shocked to see saffron selling for $647 a pound.

☺ Spend time in the fruit and vegetable section. Try to find a fruit you've never seen before. Buy it and do a taste-test at home.

☺ Make a grocery list ahead of time. Give your children the Sunday newspaper coupons and ask them to find coupons for items you need. At the store, encourage your children to find the coupon item and split the savings with you.

☺ Ask the manager for a behind-the-scenes visit. You might get to see doughnuts made or trucks delivering crates of watermelons.

☺ Read labels on cans to find out where the food came from. Your children will be amazed that some canned peaches come from Madagascar.

☺ Buy two similar items from different companies. Compare the two brands. Is the expensive roll of paper towels really more absorbent than the generic brand?

End the journey through the grocery store by giving each child a dollar to buy a special treat for themselves.

20. TV Tamers

Supplies: television set

The media constantly tell us that children watch too much television. Instead of riding bikes or catching grasshoppers, children sit mesmerized in front of the television set. Here are some ways to take control of TV time:

- ✿ Watch TV with your children. Sure, it's a great time to get chores done, but the only real way to monitor what they see is to be in the same room. When you get tired of the shows, turn them off.
- ✿ As you watch TV together, get ready for commercials. As soon as a commercial comes on, everyone has to move continuously. Jump up and down, run in place, or do sit-ups. No one gets to stop until the show begins again. You'll get a real appreciation for just how long commercials run!
- ✿ When commercials come on, push "mute" on the remote control. Select someone in the family to make up their own voice-over. This lends itself to silly dialogue.
- ✿ Pull the plug on the television and set a large, empty box in front of the screen. Tell the children that the box is their homemade TV and it's up to them to get inside and put on their own show for the rest of the family. They might even have so much fun that they'll forget about "real" TV.

21. No-Shopping Mall Walking

Supplies: shopping mall

If you live in an area where winters are cold and rainy, a trip to the mall might be just what you need. No, not an expensive shopping trip where you trudge from store to store—this trip to the mall gives everyone some much-needed exercise.

Call the closest mall and ask if they offer mall walking. The majority of malls across the country open their main doors for several hours before the shops open for people wanting to exercise in a safe, warm environment.

Some malls have regular walking programs with sign-posts along the way, telling you that twice around the mall equals one mile. Other programs give Walking Passports that get stamped after completing a certain number of miles. In most cases, you simply walk from one end of the mall to another, as often as you want. The stores are closed so you don't have to worry about hearing, "Mom, can I have that new toy?"

If you are faced with another dreary weekend, get your family up early for a few miles of power walking in the mall. Challenge children to power walk by walking briskly. Just be sure to leave before the stores open!

Extra,
Extra,
Read
All About It!

22. Reading Roundup

Supplies: reading material
Optional: costumes, paper, pencil, flashlight

No one would deny the importance of reading aloud to your child. Yet, some days it seems that everyone is too tired or too busy to read together. Here are some tips for putting pizzazz into your reading:

- Pretend you are a professional radio announcer, reading over the air. This forces you to use distinctive voices and read with dramatic flair.
- Stop reading every few pages and ask, "What do you think happens next?" "Why did Sarah want to skip school?" When children know you'll ask questions, they'll try harder to listen to the story.
- Judge a book by its cover. Spend a few minutes looking at the cover of the book. Does it look like it would be a funny book? What does the back cover tell you about the story? Compare your first impressions after reading the book.
- Ask children to be "critics." How would they rate the book on a scale of one to ten? What age group should read this book? Would they read the book again?
- Take a chance and write to the author. Many children's authors are glad to write back to young fans. There are even cases of children receiving letters from J.K. Rowling!
- Don't feel that reading must take place with a book at bedtime. Read aloud parts of the morning paper as your child eats breakfast. Read aloud the directions for chocolate chip cookies while baking with your child.
- Try round-robin reading. The family sits together and takes turns, each reading one page of the book.

Extra, Extra, Read All About It!

- Have your child read to you while you drive to soccer or wait in the dentist's office.
- Ask your child to sketch pictures about the characters in the story you are reading.
- If possible, dress as a character from the book. Put on a baggy dress and sunbonnet if reading *Little House on the Prairie*. Find a cape and pointed hat to wear during a chapter from a Harry Potter book.
- Turn out the lights and read by candlelight or firelight.
- If your children like to read under the covers with a flashlight, crawl underneath and join them!

23. Surprise Story Cards

Supplies: 4" x 6" index cards, scissors,
glue, old magazines

This activity can take place over a period of time by simply leaving the supplies available to children. They'll make new picture cards whenever they have extra time.

Set out old magazines, scissors, and glue. Provide a set of index cards as a base for your picture file. Ask your children to cut out distinct pictures of anything that catches their attention. Glue the pictures of cars, people, animals, and food to each index card. When you have a collection of twenty-five to thirty picture cards, get ready to play the game.

Give each player four or five cards, face down so they can't see the picture. The first player flips over their first card and begins making up a story, using the item on their card. Whenever she feels like it, she pauses her story and points to another player. That person flips over one of his cards and continues the story, trying to incorporate his picture. Repeat the process until everyone has used his or her cards and the story is so outlandish that it no longer makes sense.

24. Bright and Bold Book Bugs

Supplies: light cardboard or construction paper, scissors, paper fasteners (brads), markers

While some children love to read on their own, others often need subtle encouragement to pick up a book. Provide children with a visual reminder of their reading progress by making a book bug that grows with each book they read.

Let children cut four- to five-inch circles from brightly colored paper or light cardboard. An easy way to get a circle shape is to trace around a saucer or small dessert plate. After you have ten to twelve circles, punch two holes across from each other in each circle. Children find it a new experience to use paper fasteners to attach the circles together. Take two circles, overlap the edges so that two holes line up, and join them with a fastener. Continue linking circles to make a long, slinky worm.

To add to the bug effect, your child can decorate the first circle with a bug face, including eyes and antennae. Every time your child reads a book, write the title on one circle of the bug. If your child is a voracious reader, make a big fuss about adding more body parts on the bug to keep up with all of the book titles. Display your bug in a prominent place so everyone can comment on your child's reading progress.

25. Bestselling Authors

Supplies: paper or notebook, pencil

These books might not be on the bestseller's list, but they will be cherished for years to come. They also work well if you want to embarrass your children when they become teenagers.

Every year, around your child's birthday, have them write a book. Purchase a notebook or simply staple pieces of paper together. Younger children can dictate to you and add their own artwork. Older children might even use the computer for more professional results.

The title of each book should be along the lines of, "My Life As an Eight-Year-Old" or "The Year I Was Six." This gives your child a loose parameter to write about the past year of her life. A week or so before your child's birthday, encourage her to write the book, chronicling her past year. For reluctant authors, let them dictate their life story to you. The book can include names of friends or accomplishments such as making the basketball team. Keep the books in a safe place as a printed documentary of your child's growth and development. It's fun to look back with a ten-year-old at the book he wrote as a kindergartner.

26. Penmanship and Pen Pals

Supplies: paper, pencil, envelopes, stamps, stickers, markers or crayons

Letter-writing is becoming a lost form of communication. Why take the time to write a letter when you can call someone or dash off a message on email? Some schools no longer teach children to write in cursive, since fewer and fewer lessons are handwritten.

Be a trendsetter! Fight the system! Revitalize the art of writing letters! Begin by giving family members plain paper along with stickers and markers. Take a few minutes and create personalized stationery. Draw a few borders or just add stripes on the stationery side of the paper.

Have each family member select someone to write to. Older relatives make ideal pen pals. Younger children have the option of drawing pictures for Grandma. Most children will complain, "But there's nothing to write about!" Make a list of recent everyday events such as:

- The neighbor's cat had kittens.
- It was hot and everyone played in the sprinkler.
- Jackie made spaghetti for dinner.
- Everyone is going on a bike ride on Saturday.

Letters don't need to be long, just personal. Aunt Maxine will be thrilled to know Samantha took first place at the swim meet. After children finish writing, seal and mail each letter. The added benefit of this activity is that in a week you'll start getting reply letters in the mail.

27. Extra! Extra! Read All about Her!

Supplies: baseball hat, notebook, pencil, newspaper, tape

Do you have a child that needs a boost to her self-esteem? Looking for a way to make your child feel special? Brush up your journalism skills and write a front-page story about her.

Take your child aside and explain (with a twinkle in your eye) that you have a new job as a newspaper reporter. To add to the effect, wear a baseball hat with a sign reading "Reporter" on the brim. Carry an official-looking notebook also. Tell your child you'll need to interview her in order to write the feature story. Ask questions such as:

◆ What would be your perfect pet?
◆ Describe a time you helped a shy child at school.
◆ Where would you like to go on vacation?
◆ Pick five words to describe yourself.

After interviewing, type up the article about your child. Tape it on the newspaper, along with a recent photograph. Casually tell her to check out the front-page news story. Have her read the article to the rest of the family.

28. Community Book Swap

Supplies: paper and pens (or computer)
for flyers or posters, tables, books

Remember how exciting it was for your toddler to sit on your lap and pat the soft fur while you read *Pat the Bunny*? Now that your children are older, you probably have stacks of books they think are "for babies." Since your friends might be in the same situation, organize a community book sale.

Find a central location for the event. If you can't use someone's yard, ask permission to use a section of a local school playground, park, or recreation hall. Select a date and time for the sale. Call friends and ask them to spread the word that anyone can participate in selling books. Ask your children to help design a flyer publicizing the event. Distribute the flyer to local preschools or day camps, which continuously need new books. If city ordinances allow it, attach posters of the sale on telephone poles.

On the day of the event, participating families simply bring their used books to the sale and set up their miniature bookstore. Either provide folding tables or have participants bring their own. It's up to each family to price the books and handle their individual sales. Potential book buyers stroll from booth to booth, selecting books and comparing prices. Naturally, your children will quickly spend any money you make selling their books on books from another booth!

29. Group Journal

Supplies: notebook, pencil

A group journal is a great way to encourage children to record their thoughts and feelings about family activities. Purchase a notebook to take along on trips or outings. Unless you have a budding journalist in your family who is eager to do the writing, you can let the children verbalize their experiences to an adult, who does the actual writing.

When you're traveling, pull out the journal and ask questions like, "What was the funniest thing that happened last night at the campground?" "What was the best (or worst) thing about that restaurant?" or, "Who wants to describe that cool-looking house across the street from Grandma's?" With an adult writing, children are eager to share their ideas. Leave spaces for children to draw highlights of their experiences in the journal. At night, read over the previous day's adventures as a way to settle down for the evening.

Extra, Extra, Read All About It!

30. Junior Reviewers

Supplies: paper, pencils

Theater critics attend plays and then write reviews of the shows. It's soon evident if they liked the production or not. In the same way, encourage children to be junior reviewers by evaluating restaurants or attractions on a family trip.

Set up a rating system ahead of time. Ten stars might be designated for the most incredible experience of all time. A two-star rating means you'll never go back. After you visit a hotel, ask your reviewers how they would rate the stay. Was the staff friendly? Was the room clean? Did they enjoy the swimming pool?

You'll be surprised how the ratings differ. One child might give the pancake breakfast eight stars because the pancakes were in the shape of a dinosaur. Mom, however, rates the restaurant two stars because of the dirty table-cloth. One family spent two weeks visiting four major family amusement parks. After going through the rating process for the entire trip, the children gave the highest rating to the day they stumbled across a park with a small creek where they spent the afternoon building dams.

31. Jiggling Gelatin Antics

Supplies: eight to ten large boxes flavored gelatin, eight marbles, stopwatch, assorted containers

Shimmering, smooth gelatin is every child's favorite dessert. Even adults have fond memories of the way the gelatin feels sliding down your throat. Instead of just eating the gelatin, be brave and invite your family to an afternoon of outdoor gelatin antics.

Go to a discount store and find the least expensive brand of flavored gelatin. Buy at least eight to ten large boxes. Mix one box according to the directions, but cut the amount of water in half. You want this batch to be very firm. Make all the other boxes of gelatin according to the package directions. Keep the gelatin in refrigerator.

When it's time for the big event, gather your family in the backyard for some of these events:

☺ Gelatin slurp: give each participant a small glass of gelatin and a straw. Shout "GO!" and see who can slurp all the gelatin through the straw first.

☺ Set a large bowl of gelatin on the ground. Place a chair next to it. Get a stopwatch and time each person as they put a bare foot in the gelatin and try to pick up eight marbles with their toes. The fastest time is the official winner. (This is one bowl of gelatin you do not want to eat!)

☺ Bring out the extra-thick gelatin. Cut it into strips about 2" x 6". Place one strip on each participant's head and have them cross the yard while hula-hooping. It's difficult to keep the gelatin from slipping off your head as your body tries to keep the hula hoop moving.

☺ Measure to see who can throw a handful of gelatin the farthest.

Messy Projects

32. Camp-Style Body Painting

Supplies: a willing body, tempera paint and brushes, dishwashing soap

Camp counselors, with their never-ending supply of patience, allow campers to paint designs on their bodies. Think how happy you'd make your children if they could paint your body!

Get in a swimsuit or shorts and tank top. Children need as much painting area as possible. Mix several colors of tempera paint with a few drops of dishwashing soap. This helps the paint wash off easily after your body looks like a psychedelic painting.

The rest of your job is easy. Just lie out in the sun and disregard the fact that several children are painting your toes and elbows with ticklish paintbrushes. Feel free to get up if any of your children make comments about painting your many wrinkles. (Children can also happily paint each other.)

After the children are done painting, take a picture. Then find a hose to rinse off before your long, hot shower.

33. Papier-Mâché Party

Supplies: plastic container, liquid starch or wallpaper
paste, water, newspaper, paint and brushes,
old shoe, aluminum foil, balloons

There's no denying that working with papier-mâché is a messy, sticky activity. That's exactly why children love it so much. Save on cleanup by working on projects outside, where you can hose off children and tables.

Mix up a batch of papier-mâchè paste. The traditional method involves mixing flour and water that eventually hardens the paper. Two other options include:

1. Liquid Starch Formula. Mix equal amounts water and liquid starch in a plastic container. Soak strips of newspaper in the solution and use for projects.
2. Wallpaper Paste Formula. Add wallpaper paste to water until it's the consistency of tomato soup. Dip newspaper strips in the solution.

You've made the sticky solution. Now what? Here's where the fun of papier-mâché begins. Children enjoy seeing their wet, slimy pieces of paper harden in three to four hours. Wrap newspaper strips around a balloon. Let dry, and you have a great shape for a head. Paint faces and glue on yarn for the hair. Find an old shoe and wrap the soaked newspaper strips around the shoe, leaving an opening where the foot slides in. After the shoe hardens, paint it and put a small dish inside the shoe. Add water and flowers for a one-of-a-kind vase. Use aluminum foil to create a base for a dinosaur. Cover foil with layers of soaked newspaper strips to create a solid, fierce dinosaur. Once your children see how the layered, wet newspapers turn into a sturdy form, you'll be amazed at what they'll want to transform with papier-mâché!

34. Silly Finger Painting

Supplies: surgical glove, acrylic paint, large
pieces of paper or cardboard, needle

Most people connect painting with paintbrushes. Yet many other objects work to get paint onto the canvas. Maybe your children have done sponge or finger painting. Have they ever painted with a surgical glove?

For obvious reasons, you'll be better off trying this activity outside where paint drips absorb into the grass. Have several colors of thin paint available. Place paper or cardboard on a flat surface. Since it's a surprise where the paint ends up, the bigger the pieces of paper, the better.

Hand your child a surgical glove. Have them hold it open while you pour in about a half cup of paint, trying to fill at least one rubber finger. Gather the excess glove together, forcing the paint to the bottom of the fingers. Hold the glove over the paper. An adult pokes a hole with a needle into the fingertip of the glove.

You know what happens next. A steady stream of paint flows from the hole onto the paper. See if children can write their names or draw a specific shape. Continue the process with other colors of paint. Cleanup is simple: toss the gloves away. This is one time you don't want to recycle.

35. Mystery Slime

Supplies: large bowl, 1 cup water, 2 cups cornstarch
Optional: food coloring, spatulas

Don't worry, this Mystery Slime is harmless. Your children (and yourself) will spend long hours playing with this "stuff" that is part liquid and part solid. You have to have it ooze through your fingers to fully understand how much fun it is.

The only two ingredients you'll need are cornstarch and water. Since children like to really get their hands in the Mystery Slime, use a dishpan or large bowl for the container. Stir the water and cornstarch together until it gets thick and oozy. At that point, the fun begins. Have children reach their hands into the Mystery Slime and try to pick it up. At first, they'll have a firm mass of slime, which then slowly begins to ooze through their fingers. Take a fist and pound on the slime. It hardens, and then softens almost instantly.

Watch what happens when you add a few drops of food coloring. The swirls of color magically start to blend into the Mystery Slime. Use spoons or rubber spatulas to have even more fun scooping up this strange substance.

36. Messy, Moldy Masks

Supplies: eggs, coffee grounds, hair dryer

The next time that your children want to play dress-up, suggest that they make some messy masks. (They'll wonder why you aren't telling them to *not* make a mess.) Since this activity gets drippy, it's best to do it over a sink or an area with a washable floor.

Show the children how to separate the egg yolk from the egg white. Let the children break two or three eggs, collecting only the egg white in a plastic bowl. (Discard the yolks or reserve for another use.) Beat the egg whites lightly with a fork. Make "mosaic" pieces from the eggshells by crushing them into small pieces. Collect a small bowl of coffee grounds, also.

Here's the gooey part: you start by smearing the egg white over your face. Gently press on the eggshells, creating a mosaic mask. If you want to look like you're growing a beard, pat coffee grounds into the sides and chin area of your face. Use a hair dryer set on low to briefly dry the egg white on your face.

Look in the mirror and see your messy mask. It actually seems to glow in the dark when you're in a dark room with a flashlight shining on your face.

37. Slippery Slimy Goop

Supplies: 1 cup cold water, 1 cup white school glue,
1 tablespoon borax (such as 20 Mule Team Borax,
found in the laundry section of most grocery stores),
1/2 cup hot water, 2 mixing bowls
Optional: food coloring

Be careful with this next project. You may find this substance so much fun to play with that you will take it to work to amaze your coworkers. They'll all be asking for the recipe, so be prepared to hand it out.

Follow these easy directions for hours of fun. Combine cold water with white school glue and mix well. In a separate bowl, mix borax with very hot (but not boiling) water. If you wish, add a few drops of food coloring to the borax mixture. Slowly add the borax mixture to the glue mixture. Stir for a few minutes and the substance will turn into a stretchy, smooth, slimy substance. Knead it on a kitchen counter until very smooth.

It's difficult to explain the calming effect Goop has on children. They'll smile while spreading it or letting it flow through their fingers. The Goop returns back to its basic smooth shape and always remains cool to the touch. When you get done playing with it, store it in a plastic bag in the refrigerator for another day of fun.

38. Totally Awesome Toes

Supplies: toes, washable markers

If your children have toes, they can do this activity anytime, anywhere. Well, maybe not in the middle of a wedding ceremony, but almost anywhere.

Begin with bare feet. Since you'll be decorating toes, socks and shoes need to be removed. Take a good look at the bottom of your toes. Have you noticed that they are shaped like little faces? It's time those blank faces developed some personality.

Set out a variety of washable markers. Ask your child if you can draw a face on the bottom of his big toe. Outline the entire toe to get distinct face shapes. Be prepared for giggles! The markers sometimes reduce children to a fit of laughter. Since children are so flexible, have them draw on their toes themselves.

After you have funny faces on the bottom of your feet, sing some songs and wiggle your toes as part of the "Smelly Feet Choir."

39. Groovy Body Glitter

Supplies: small containers such as baby food jars
or pint canning jars, paint or permanent markers,
mixing bowl and spoon, 1 cup aloe vera gel,
1 teaspoon glycerin, 2-3 teaspoons glitter

You'd probably faint if your child came home covered with tattoos or body piercings. To keep peace in the family, encourage children to make body glitter and spread that on their skin instead of something permanent.

Collect a variety of small jars. Use paint or permanent markers to decorate each one. After all, you want the containers to look just as nice as the ones in specialty shops.

In a bowl, thoroughly mix aloe vera gel and glycerin. (Both can be found in drug stores.) Add glitter or tiny metal confetti. Scoop mixture into the decorated jars. Chill in refrigerator for several hours. Label so that no one thinks it's a snack!

When children want their bodies to shimmer, spread the body glitter on cheeks, knees, elbows, stomach, etc.

Messy Projects

40. Fantastic Face Paint

Supplies: small bowls, measuring spoons,
1 tablespoon cornstarch, 1 1/2 teaspoons
cold cream, 1 1/2 teaspoon water,
food coloring, cotton swabs or
small paintbrushes

Face-painting is a popular event at children's carnivals or festivals. Usually there are long lines of children waiting to get unicorns drawn on their chubby cheeks. The following easy recipe lets you keep a steady supply of face paint on hand. (Make a little extra money by telling children you'll paint their faces for a small fee!)

Begin by mixing the basic recipe and then divide it into three bowls for different colors. Mix together cornstarch and cold cream. Slowly stir in water until mixture is thick and smooth. Spoon the white face paint into three containers. Add one or two drops of food coloring to each bowl and mix well. Add a few drops more color if you want darker face paint.

Use cotton swabs or small paintbrushes to paint designs on faces. Sit children in front of a mirror and let them paint their own faces. Be really brave and let them paint your face!

41. Foolish Fake Blood

Supplies: mixing bowl, measuring cup and tablespoon,
5 tablespoons cornstarch, 1/3 cup water,
2/3 cup corn syrup, food coloring

There comes a time in every child's life when they must have some fake blood. Maybe he wants to scare his little sister, or use it at a Halloween party. When Steven Spielberg was twelve, he needed fake blood for a home movie. His mother patiently mixed batches of various liquids together in the blender, trying to get just the right consistency. If only she had this recipe!

In a bowl, mix together water and cornstarch. Stir until smooth. Add corn syrup and mix well. You now have the correct consistency for blood.

Slowly add two to four drops red food coloring. You'll get a bright red mixture. For a more realistic appearance, add one or two drops of green food coloring. This makes the blood look darker. Now figure out how to scare people with your concoction!

Messy Projects

Cool
Things
to Make

42. Laughing Luminaries

*Supplies: brown paper lunch bags, scissors, sand,
votive candles, long wooden matches*

It's a magical experience to walk up a driveway and see a
row of paper bags glowing softly (and safely) with candlelight. Traditionally, people set out luminaries during winter
holidays, but you can use them anytime you want to add a
festive atmosphere. Luminaries are safe, but should never
be left unattended.

Gather ten or twelve brown paper lunch bags. Leaving
three or four inches at the bottom, children can sketch a
laughing face or design on each bag and then cut it out.
Some children enjoy just cutting various designs in the bag
without any preset pattern. After the bags have cuts to
allow the light to shine through, take them outside. For
extra stability, fold the top edge over about one inch. Fill
each bag with at least three or four inches of sand. Space
the bags along a sidewalk or up a driveway. Press a votive
candle firmly in the sand in the very center of each bag.

Have an adult use a long wooden match to light each
candle. Unless it is very windy, the candles burn until they
run out of wax. At that point the flame puts itself out in the
sand. Keep the paper bags filled with sand and simply add
new candles whenever you want to add some light to a
dark evening.

43. Crafty Coded Messages

Supplies: paper, cotton swabs, small bowl, 1 tablespoon lemon juice, 1/2 tablespoon water, lamp

Remember what fun it was to write notes to your friends in a secret code you developed? Usually the message was no more involved than "Call me tonight," but because it was written in code, the words took on great importance.

Instead of using a code, write invisible messages that "magically" appear on plain paper. Give your children paper and cotton swabs. These are their writing tools. Mix together one tablespoon of lemon juice and a half tablespoon of water in a small bowl.

Have children dip the swab in the lemon juice and begin writing on the paper. After the message is complete, let the paper dry. Give the paper to the intended recipient. Naturally, they'll wonder why you gave them a blank piece of paper.

Here's the secret method for displaying the message. Hold the paper very close to a light bulb. Within seconds, the lemon juice letters start to turn brown, revealing the top-secret message.

44. Giant Body Silhouettes

Supplies: large roll of butcher paper or bulletin board paper from a school-supply store, scissors, markers

Most elementary school students have traced their bodies on a large piece of paper. The following activity adds a warm-fuzzy aspect to this simple art experience.

Get a large roll of butcher paper and lay it on a hard floor. (If you live near a newspaper printer, you can often get the ends of plain newsprint rolls for free.) Take turns tracing around each family member's body. (Somehow the heads always turn out squashed-looking, but that simply adds to the fun.) Set out crayons or markers and decorate your body, adding details for hair, facial features, and clothes. When everyone's body is complete, exchange paper "bodies" with each other. Use a dark marker and write several positive characteristics about the person you have. Think of comments such as, "Jennifer wakes up in a good mood," or, "Dad plays catch with me even if he is tired." Keep exchanging paper bodies until everyone has written comments on each family member.

Even though these bodies are large, hang them in a prominent location for a few days. Everyone will enjoy reading the positive comments.

Cool Things to Make

45. Variations on Homemade Play Dough

Supplies: saucepan, 2 cups water, food coloring (paste or liquid), 2 cups flour, 1 cup salt, 3 tablespoons vegetable oil, 1 tablespoon cream of tartar

Some parents enjoy baking cookies with their children, having delightful conversations while carefully measuring ingredients. Other parents find that cookie baking involves a mess and frequent loud reminders of, "Don't eat the dough! It has raw eggs in it!" Instead of adding stress and extra calories to your diet, let children have a "doughy" experience by making batches of homemade play dough. They'll get to measure, knead, poke, and play with the dough, while you relax.

An adult needs to bring water to a boil. After that, children can easily follow directions and make the dough on their own.

1. Boil water in a medium saucepan.
2. Stir in two to three drops food coloring. (Cake-decorating-paste color works best, but ordinary liquid food coloring will produce colored dough.)
3. Mix in flour, salt, oil, and cream of tartar (keep looking, it's probably in the very back of your spice cupboard).
4. Keep stirring until the mixture is the consistency of mashed potatoes.
5. Plop the mixture on the kitchen counter and let cool before children handle.
6. Knead the dough for five to seven minutes. If very sticky, sprinkle a small amount of flour on the counter and knead it into the dough.
7. Give your children plastic knives, cookie cutters, and rolling pins to create soft and pliable creatures. When the fun is done, store dough in a resealable plastic bag in the refrigerator.

A few variations:

○ Sprinkle glitter on the counter and knead the dough in it for a sparkly effect.

○ Add a few drops of vanilla, peppermint, or lemon oil to the boiling water. Your dough will have a pleasant scent.

○ If your children are tired of the dough color, add a few drops of food coloring to the prepared dough. As the children mix in the color, the dough takes on a swirled effect and then eventually changes to another color.

46. Popsicle Stick Puzzles

Supplies: wooden Popsicle sticks, tape, markers, resealable plastic bag

Back when today's grown-ups went to camp, many craft projects involved gluing wooden Popsicle sticks together. Younger campers glued the sticks around cans for pencil holders only a mother could love. Older campers advanced to making lopsided birdcages from hundreds of Popsicle sticks.

Today, the wooden sticks are sold inexpensively in hobby stores. Even if you are not crafty, here's an easy way to make a wooden puzzle. Lay out ten to twelve sticks side by side on a flat surface. Take a piece of tape and run it across one end of all the sticks so they stay together. Do the same across the other end of the sticks. Turn the sticks over so the taped side is underneath.

Using crayons or markers, draw a picture on the sticks. Make it as colorful and detailed as you want, making sure to color on all of the sticks. When the picture is complete, remove the tape and mix up the sticks. Ask a friend to try to rearrange the stick puzzle so the picture is once again intact. Store the sticks in a resealable plastic bag to use over and over again.

47. Favorite Shirt-Turned-Pillow

Supplies: T-shirt; cotton batting (found in craft or sewing departments); sewing machine; needle and thread, or fabric glue

Every child has a favorite T-shirt that he'd wear daily if you didn't sneak it away to get washed. The time comes, however, when that shirt just won't fit your growing child anymore. Turn a cherished piece of clothing into a sentimental pillow.

Wash the T-shirt or sweatshirt and turn it inside out. Since this will be a pillow, the seams need to be closed. This might be a good time to show your child how to use a sewing machine. Sew together the neck, bottom edge, and the end of one sleeve. This is great practice for children to learn how to sew by hand with a needle and thread. The straight edges are forgiving to crooked stitches. Craft stores sell heavy-duty fabric glue that closes seams as well.

After the sewing is completed, turn the shirt right side out. Stuff cotton batting into the shirt through the one sleeve opening. Smooth the batting in the neck and sleeve area. Get the pillow nice and plump. When the pillow is as soft as you want it, hand sew the last opening on the arm. This special T-shirt pillow can be a part of your child's life for many years to come.

48. Anytime Sand Castles

Supplies: plastic containers such as yogurt or margarine tubs, cooking oil spray, playground sand (can be purchased at home improvement stores), 2 1/2 cups cornstarch, 1 1/2 tablespoons cream of tartar, 3 cups hot water, stove, large saucepan, measuring cups and spoons

If you live in Kansas or Oklahoma, your children don't get to spend their afternoons at the beach. Instead of wishing you were near an ocean, make your own building blocks for year-round sand castles in the backyard.

Send children on a search of the house, looking for empty plastic containers like margarine or yogurt tubs. Plastic ice cube trays also work well. Lightly spray the inside of each container with cooking oil spray. This helps release the sand mold.

Measure four cups playground sand. This can be purchased at home improvement stores. (If you happen to live on a tropical island with plenty of sand, use that!) Pour the sand into a large saucepan. Add cornstarch and cream of tartar and mix well. Pour in hot water. Have an adult stir the mixture over medium heat until it starts to get very stiff, about four or five minutes. Let cool just until it's safe to handle.

Scoop the sand mixture into your molds. Pack firmly and let dry overnight. The next day, unmold your mix-and-match sand shapes. They'll be firm and great for stacking on top of each other to make fantasy sand castles anytime.

49. Homemade Scratch-and-Sniff

Supplies: paper or plain labels, generic unsweetened
powdered drink mix, water, paintbrush,
plastic film canisters

Stickers of any kind are fun, but even more fun when you can scratch and sniff. (Some manufacturer actually made a "dirty sock" scratch-and-sniff sticker! Let's hope it wasn't a bestseller.) These special stickers allow you to scratch with a fingernail to release the smell of fresh strawberry or lemon.

It's easy enough to make your own scratch-and-stiff stickers. Begin with plain address labels or even plain paper. Purchase generic unsweetened powdered drink mix. You'll need different flavors for different scents.

Mix together one tablespoon of powdered drink mix with one tablespoon of very warm water. Stir well until the powder is dissolved. Use this mixture with a regular craft paintbrush to paint a design on the sticker or paper. Let dry overnight. The next morning, scratch the dried paint with your finger to release the smell. Mix up several different flavors and store in empty plastic film canisters. Paint different stickers and try to guess the smell. Let's hope it's not dirty socks!

50. Crafty Chain of Events

Supplies: paper, blunt scissors, pencil, glue or tape

The holidays wouldn't be complete without seeing a paper chain, dripping with glue, made by a proud kindergartner. Take the same chain concept and use it as a way to pass time on the next trip.

Ask children to cut forty to fifty paper strips about 1" x 6". Don't worry if they aren't all precision cut. Before children glue the ends to make an ordinary chain, turn the papers into an extraordinary activity. On each slip of paper, write a simple task that can be done in a car or plane such as, "Count backwards from fifty to one." Other activities could be:

- Sing "The Star Spangled Banner."
- Comb your hair into a new style.
- Draw a picture of the perfect snack food.
- Write a short poem about another family member.
- Describe a stuffed animal you have and see if others can guess what it is.
- What would you do if you found a $100 bill under your seat?
- Get the family saying any tongue twisters you know.

Naturally all the ideas need to be doable in a confined space. If you need more ideas to put on the paper strips, ask children for suggestions. Glue or tape the paper into a chain, interlocking each piece. Take the chain along on your next trip. When children get restless, pull out the chain and let each child remove a link and perform the activity.

51. Plaster Molds

Supplies: sand (purchased or from the beach),
1 1/2 cups plaster of paris (the least expensive
brand at the hardware store), 2 cups water,
disposable plastic bowl or coffee can, stir
stick, shells, plastic animals, paint, brushes

Making molds in the sand is a great beach activity. If you don't live close to the ocean, it's easy to make your own portable "beach in a bucket." Simply purchase playground sand from a hardware store and pour it into a large plastic dishpan or bucket. Instant beach!

Collect a variety of shells, plastic dinosaurs, or other items with distinct shapes. Set them aside as you prepare the sand. It needs to be damp, but not too runny. A spray bottle with water helps gently moisten the sand. Pack the sand firmly. For best results, spray the item you want to imprint with a light coating of spray cooking oil. This helps release the item from the sand. Firmly press the item into the sand. Lift it up to reveal a distinct impression. Repeat as often as you like with different items.

It's also fun to get a person with big feet to step firmly on the dampened sand, especially with their toes. To make an extra-big footprint, have the person keep their toes in one spot but slide their foot from side, and gently lift up on the toes and push the foot back, lengthening the heel area. You should now have a fat, long footprint in the sand.

Mix together the water with the plaster of paris in a disposable container. Stir well until it has the consistency of a milkshake. Gently pour the plaster into the sand molds. Let set for several hours. Remove the hardened plaster shapes and brush off the sand. Paint your shells or animals with acrylic paint.

Cool Things to Make

In High Gear

52. Sprinting Ducks

Supplies: doorway, pillows, balls or sponges

Have you ever been to a shooting gallery at a carnival and watched the little mechanical ducks rapidly travel back and forth, avoiding getting shot? This game gets family members moving, trying to avoid getting hit with small balls or pillows.

Select an area of the house that has a door with wall space on both sides. Family members sit in one room, while someone in the next room runs back and forth in front of the door, just like the ducks at the carnival. Family members take turns throwing small foam balls or sponges at the human "duck." There's something highly amusing about seeing an adult throw his body across the doorway to avoid getting tagged by a ball. If a ball hits the person, they sit down and the ball thrower gets to be the next duck. To add to the fun, insist that the person running has to continuously make quacking sounds.

To change the pace, try throwing large pillows instead of small balls.

53. Super Slider

Supplies: hardwood or tile floor, carpet square or small throw rug, tape measure

Some parents cringe at the thought of playing active games inside the house. This activity satisfies children's urge to scoot around while keeping furniture in one piece.

Select a hallway or large room with a smooth floor. Hardwood, tile, or linoleum floors all work fine. Set up a starting line and give the first "slider" a carpet square or small throw rug. The carpet piece goes on the starting line as your child moves back, gets a running start, and hops on the rug, knees first. The object is to see who can slide the farthest. Have a tape measure handy to record the distance of each competitor. For variety, children can slide sitting down or even on their stomachs. For safety reasons, discourage children from sliding while standing on the carpet square.

Adults can get into the fun by sliding also. You may not get the momentum to break the distance record, but you will be a winner in your child's eyes as you glide down the hall and crash into a wall!

54. Silly Suitcase Race

Supplies: large flat playing area, suitcases, assorted clothing

Kids love relay races. Add a comical touch to this tried-and-true favorite with outlandish costumes.

Fill two suitcases or backpacks with clothing. Try to make the items in each bag similar. If one pair of pants has an elastic waist, make sure the other pair does also. Avoid clothing with lots of buttons, which are frustrating for young fingers to fasten in a hurry. Loose-necked, slipover sweatshirts work best, along with silly items like fluffy petticoats.

After the bags are packed, line everyone up in two teams at the starting line. Set the suitcases about fifteen to twenty feet from the starting line. On "go!" the first person in each line races to their designated suitcase and frantically puts on the assorted pieces of clothing. They run back to their teammate waiting in line and undress. As soon as an item of clothing comes off, the waiting teammate can put it on. That teammate then runs to the empty suitcase and undresses. He/she races to the next waiting child and tags them. The race continues with children dressing and undressing. The first team to have all their members participate is declared the Silly Suitcase winner.

If you have a large number of children, try to have four or five lines of children (with four or five suitcases). Otherwise the lines are too long and children end up losing interest because they've had to wait too long.

55. Tag! You're It!

Supplies: large flat playing area
Optional: flashlight, broom, popcorn, ballet music

Channel children's natural desire to run and shout by organizing several versions of the game of tag. Once they get started, ask them to come up with their own versions. You may start a whole new craze!

It's usually best to set boundaries for the play area. Here a few popular versions of tag:

- ☺ Cartoon tag: the person who is "it" chases the others. If she tags someone, that person remains frozen until another player comes along, taps her and says the name of a cartoon character.
- ☺ Double tag: everyone gets a partner and links arms. Pick a team to be "It." These two chase the other partners. For example, Jason and Michael are running away from "It." Michael gets tagged. That means his partner, Jason is free to run away from "It". The only way to be safe is hook up with Seth and Emily. When Jason grabs Emily's arm, Seth takes off running.
- ☺ Flashlight Tag: at night, give "It" a flashlight. Children run and hide behind trees or shrubs (within a designated area). "It" yells out, "Back to base!" Everyone tries to sneak back to the designated base area without getting "tagged" by the flashlight's beam of light.
- ☺ Shadow Tag: try this on a sunny day. Children race around, trying to avoid "It." If "It" steps on a person's shadow, that person becomes "It" and tries to catch someone else.
- ☺ Broom Tag: the person who is "It" carries a broom. As soon as he tags someone, that person joins "It" by holding on to the broom. Now two people are chasing others. As soon as they tag

another person, that child joins the "Broom Gang." Continue playing until there is no more room to hold on to the broom.

☺ Popcorn Tag: instead of running, everyone has to hop like a kernel of popcorn. When "It" tags someone, that person hooks up behind "It," holding on to "It's" waist. Now the double kernel has to stay together and hop after someone else. If either person tags another child, that child joins the growing bunch of popcorn. If the group is very large, sub-divide the popcorn groups after they reach five or six children; too large a group gets cumbersome as they hop around chasing loose kernels. Afterward, serve popcorn for a snack.

☺ Ballet Tag: combine the grace of a ballerina with the exuberance of children. If any participants have had ballet lessons, let them demonstrate the plié or arabesque, etc. Ballet music is an integral part of this game. Everyone must move by dancing in time to the music—no running is allowed. Making up pretend ballet moves is okay (and quite amusing). If the music is slow, children must move very slowly; when the music speeds up, everyone dances as fast as they can, on their toes, arms swaying gently overhead. When "It" tags someone, that person becomes "It" and dances over to tag another child.

56. Gooley Gooley

Supplies: large flat playing area

Children love the spontaneity of this game because there are few rules involved. It's simply a chance to get all excited and be with friends. Adults, however, need to have a strong voice to be heard above the yells of children.

Gather the group in a semi-contained area to explain the game. Everyone raises their hands in the air and starts saying, "Gooley, gooley, gooley..." while moving around in a random fashion. An adult shouts out a number such as "FIVE!" Children immediately grab at each other and try to sit down in groups of five. Rather than eliminate people, if a group has the "wrong" number, just proceed with the game. Have everyone stand and begin milling around saying, "Gooley gooley..." etc. If you have a large group, call out a high number such as "twelve!" and watch the excitement as groups try to add and subtract people to get the correct number.

For variety, have children raise hands in the air and hop or skip around while saying "gooley". Try calling out "one!" and watch as people automatically grab a partner.

57. Flying Frisbee Golf

Supplies: large play area, trees or other uprights,
paper plates, markers, thumbtacks, Frisbees

Wouldn't your child like to be the undisputed champion of Frisbee golf? Who says you have to have an eighteen-hole golf course?

Get children involved by asking them to decorate as many paper plates as you want "holes" for your golf course (twelve is usually enough). Number each plate from one to twelve with a large black number in the center. This will tell the players where to throw the Frisbee next. Find a large area in a park, or if you are fortunate, your backyard. Children need room to throw the Frisbee without danger of hitting a window.

Begin with plate No. 1 and tack it to a tree or other safe target. From there, find another "target" about ten feet away and attach plate No. 2. Continue until all the plates are distributed around the area. Get creative and put up a target behind a sprinkler so the Frisbee needs to go through water.

Give the first child a Frisbee and have them try to hit the No. 1 target. If they miss, they simply pick up the Frisbee where it landed and try to hit the No. 1 target from that point. When they finally touch target No. 1, they go on to find No. 2. In the meantime, another child can start playing. It's all right if they pass each other while throwing the Frisbees. It's more fun to see several Frisbees flying around anyway. This is a low-key activity because children can stop or start whenever they want. No need to keep score since the fun is simply trying to hit the targets in order.

58. Sand Bowling

Supplies: sandy beach, ball, ten plastic liter
bottles, two or more players

The next time you go to the beach, pack ten empty plastic liter bottles along with the sunscreen. They're bulky, but the fun your children will have bowling in the sand makes up for any inconvenience. Include a beach ball or volleyball and your outdoor bowling alley is complete.

Select an area of the beach out of the main traffic flow. You don't want people walking through your bowling pins just as you're making a strike. Set up a triangle shape with the bottles, starting with a row of four bottles about four to six inches apart. Push them down slightly into the sand. In front of that row, line up a row of three bottles, and then a row of two. Add one bottle for the top of your triangle and begin bowling.

Draw a line in the sand about fifteen feet from the "pins." Stand behind the line and roll the ball, trying to knock down as many pins as possible. Each child gets two tries. Children soon begin experimenting with the weight of the bottles. What happens if each bottle is partially filled with sand? Will a beach ball knock over a bottle filled with water? Children have just as much fun filling the bottles with combinations of water and sand as they do actually bowling.

An easy variation of this game is simply to dig holes in the sand instead of using bottles. Dig ten holes in the same triangular pattern. Give a point value to each hole. Children roll the ball, aiming for the hole worth the most points.

59. Beach Ball Obstacle Course

Supplies: large, flat playing area, beach balls, plastic milk jugs, garbage cans, hula hoops, boxes, boards, etc.

Colorful, lightweight beach balls provide an ideal prop for outdoor activities. Many dollar stores feature various sizes for the amazing price of...one dollar! Enlist the help of your children to blow up the balls. Otherwise you'll find yourself light-headed and unable to join in the frivolity.

Ask the children to help you set up an obstacle course. They'll have a great time collecting plastic milk jugs, garbage cans, and hula hoops for the course. Designate a start and finish line, while the children design the rest of the course. It's up to them to create a course where participants kick a beach ball around a tree, through a hanging hula hoop, up a ramp, into a box...you get the idea. Children usually have just as much fun making the obstacle course as actually participating in the event.

After you've inspected the course for safety, let the games begin! Line up children and let them go one at a time, kicking the ball through the course. Often, children simply want to do the course several times, without thinking about "winning". If your group is on the competitive side, time each child and record who completes the course in the fastest time. Feel free to vary the event by having your children complete the course by crab-walking and kicking the ball or attempting the course with a semi-deflated ball between their knees. They'll probably come up with numerous variations on their own.

60. Terrific Tree Tag

Supplies: more trees than children

There are two main requirements for this game: energetic children and at least ten to twelve trees, preferably more trees than children. Begin by designating boundary areas so children don't get lost in the deep, dark woods.

Each child stands by a tree. One person is designated "It." To avoid squabbles over who gets to be "It" first, ask something like, "Who has a birthday coming up?" The person with the next birthday receives the honor of starting the game.

"It" stands in the center of the trees and shouts, "Terrific Tree Tag!" Everyone runs to another tree as "It" tries to tag someone who is not touching a tree. There can only be one person per tree, so split-second decisions need to be made as two runners converge on a single tree. If "It" tags someone, that person now is "It" and calls out "Terrific Tree Tag" as everyone else scrambles for a new tree. If you are lucky enough to be in an area where trees are spread out, this is a wonderful way to get children worn out from running.

61. Balloon Broom Hockey

Supplies: large flat playing area, brooms, balloons, buckets or boxes for goals

Looking for an activity that keeps everyone moving? Need to keep children of various ages involved? Collect some brooms and get ready to make a clean sweep playing broom hockey. Ask visiting children ahead of time to bring brooms. This saves you from having to go door-to-door, borrowing them.

Select a large playing area where you can set up two goals at each end. This doesn't have to be fancy. Two buckets about ten feet apart make great goals. If someone has portable soccer goals, put those to use. Since this game involves balloons, a grassy area works best. If you use a paved area, mylar balloons are best because latex pops too easily.

After the goals are in place, divide the group into two equal teams of about eight to ten children each. Don't worry about the exact number—the rules of Balloon Broom Hockey are very relaxed. If a child wants to play, and you have a broom, put her on the field!

Have a box of inflated balloons available. Have the two teams line up on the field, brooms in hand, and drop an inflated balloon mid-field. The goal is for Team No. 1 to use their broom to bat the balloon through Team No. 2's goal. Balloons have a mind of their own and move in unpredictable ways, so athletic skill doesn't matter. If the balloon pops, toss in another one and resume play. The game ends when the children lose interest.

62. Bicycle Obstacle Course

Supplies: large flat playing area, bicycles, boxes, cones, chalk, etc.

In some neighborhoods, local police officers conduct bicycle obstacle courses. They arrive with all the safety cones, props, and equipment to set up a course that tests children's bicycle-handling skills. In other neighborhoods, parents are left with the task of setting up a course. It isn't as hard as it sounds.

A flat, car-free area is essential. School play areas or a neighborhood cul-de-sac that has been blocked off provide plenty of room for the obstacle course. Make sure to stress safety and insist that all bike-riders wear helmets.

Here are some ideas for activities:

◆ Assign several parents the task of each coming up with one activity. It could be having children ride their bikes on a curvy chalk line or challenging riders to ride a straight line between two rows of raw eggs. This saves you work and the other parents get to show off their ingenuity!

◆ Set up start and finish lines about twenty feet apart and have "The World's Slowest Bicycle Race." The goal is to go as slowly as possible to the finish line without putting your foot on the ground for balance. It's great watching normally daredevil, high energy children try to balance on a bike that is barely moving.

◆ Announce in advance that there will be a Best Decorated Bike contest. Some children will come just for the chance to show off their bike covered with foil, balloons, and streamers.

◆ Instead of one long obstacle course, set up several shorter ones with trashcans and safety cones. If several mini-courses are set up, children have more chances to participate.

63. Wacky Softball

Supplies: large flat playing area; bat; softball; two door-mats, car floor mats, sandbags, or old carpet squares for home plate and a single base

Ever try playing softball with a group ranging from preschoolers to senior citizens? When younger children finally hit the ball they run randomly on the field, totally unaware what it means to "run to first!" Competitive teenagers complain because they can't demonstrate their athletic ability. Try playing Wacky Softball instead, where the rules allow everyone to have fun.

Begin on a large level playing field. Divide into two teams, eight to ten people per team. (See, the rules are very loose.) Instead of confusing people with three bases, simply set up one base about thirty-five feet behind the pitcher's mound.

The game goes like this:

- Basically you play like regular softball except there are no foul balls, strikes or balls, or basemen, and only one base.
- One team scatters all around the playing field to play "outfield." Any ball is a fair ball, even in the opposing team's dugout.
- The pitcher throws the ball to the first batter. If she doesn't hit the ball, she keeps trying until she does. When she hits the ball, she runs to the single base. She's out if the opposing team catches the ball, or retrieves the ball and throws to someone who tags her out.
- Batter No. 2 steps to the plate and hits the ball. He runs to the base also. Depending on where the ball was hit, batter No. 1 might either run home or decide to stay on the base. Hey, that's OK!
- You might end up with five people on the base. They may all decide to run home at the same

time, or maybe only two people run home. The score could be 4 to 1 when suddenly seven people on base run in together, changing the score to 11 to 1.

This is a chance for a preschooler and his grandpa to be on base together and hold hands while running for home plate.

64. Giant-Sized Softball

Supplies: large flat playing area; beach ball;
hula hoop; foam swim noodle; four doormats,
car floor mats, sandbags, or old carpet
squares for home plate and three bases

Playing baseball or softball is part of American culture. The smell of the hot dogs, children racing around bases, outfielders catching fly balls...it's all part of the game. Yet even the best games can be changed for variety.

The next time your gang is near an open field, try playing Giant-Sized Softball. If a giant were playing softball, what would he use for a ball? That's right! A beach ball. Set up the game as you would for traditional softball. You need a flat playing area to set up the three bases. Bring them closer to home plate, since beach balls don't travel as far as softballs. Oh yes, a few more props are needed. Your giant-sized bat is a foam swim noodle. Watch what happens when the noodle hits the beach ball! In the outfield, players need a hula hoop. When the beach ball comes flying towards them, they "catch" it as best they can with the hula hoop (depending on the relative size, the ball might go right through), and then throw the ball.

Instead of racing around the bases, runners must skip from base to base. Other than those few changes, this is just another game of All-American softball. It works especially well with mixed age groups, since athletic ability is not a top requirement.

65. Basketball with Adoring Fans

Supplies: basketball court or large flat playing area, basketball, adults

The next time you have a large group of children and adults, try playing this adaptation of basketball. It's as much fun for the spectators as it is for the players.

Divide the children into two teams as if you were playing regular basketball. So far, so good. Now have a parent (or stand-in adult) for each player come on the court and hold onto the back waistband of their child's pants.

Children play basketball, trying to disregard the fact that their parent is running along with them at all times. Children twist and turn, trying to shoot baskets while parents try not to get in the way. This is especially amusing to watch when twelve-year-old boys play and their mothers are frantically trying to keep up. During one particularly intense game, one mother got several warnings for actually trying to grab the ball from the opposing team!

The same concept works just as well for playing soccer or baseball. One group of children set out a very strict rule: moms *were not* allowed to kiss their children on the playing field!

66. Tricycle Triathalon

Supplies: tricycles, boxes, eggs, swim noodles

By the time children reach elementary school age, they ride bikes with confidence—sometimes too much confidence, as they leap curbs and perform other daredevil stunts. Help them relive their early childhood by organizing tricycle races.

The hardest part of this event is rounding up at least five trikes for the races. Once you've collected trikes from parents of preschoolers, try some of these events:

- Set up an obstacle course with funny obstacles. Stand shoeboxes on end and place an egg on top. Young drivers ride around the boxes, being careful not to break any eggs.
- Place a foam swim noodle on the backs of two chairs. The children must ride the trikes underneath without knocking down the noodle.
- Use the same obstacle course but blindfold the trike rider. A friend walks nearby and gives verbal instructions on how to navigate the course.
- Have a "drag strip" for teams to race relay-style to the end of a line and back.
- Draw a wavy chalk line on a driveway or pavement area. Time the children to see how fast they can ride their tricycle from the beginning to the end of the line.
- Have several relay race events where the children ride trikes to a designated area and perform certain tasks. They could pick up a goofy hat to wear, or figure out how to carry a beach ball while riding the trike back to their team member.
- Set up a course where riders weave in and out of chairs with a plastic bowl of water on their head.

67. Grab the Stinger

Supplies: large flat playing area, wide black
ribbon or sock, plastic headbands,
chenille stems (pipe cleaners)

Any time children gather outdoors, they look for reasons to run and chase each other. Put a spin on plain old games of tag by having children chase each other in groups. Since children will be running without always seeing ahead of them, make sure the playing field is level and free from obstructions.

Divide children into groups of at least eight kids. Line each team up, one behind the other. Each child holds the waist of the child in front of them. Pretend you are making an extra-large bumblebee. To add to the illusion, make bumblebee antennae by adding chenille stems to plastic headbands. (The craft industry is trying hard to change the term "pipe cleaner" to "chenille stem," so we'll be politically correct from now on.) The first person in each line wears the headband.

Walk to the end of the lines and tuck a black sock or piece of fabric into the waist of the last child on each team. This is their stinger. On "go," the teams start running and "buzzing." You should hear a continuous "buzz buzz buzz." The teams run with two objectives. The first person in each team wants to grab the stinger from an opposing team. At the same time, the last person in line has to make sure no one grabs her stinger. Keeping connected, the lines simultaneously chase other teams while avoiding being chased. As soon as a team grabs a stinger, rotate positions so everyone gets a chance to wear the bee headband or have the stinger attached to their pants.

68. Tag That Tail

Supplies: at least two children, unobstructed play area,
18" strip of crepe paper or fabric, chalk or rope

Here's an activity that combines movement, speed, and strategy. Children of mixed ages can play because size is not a factor.

Designate a smooth playing area, free from rocks or obstructions. Grass works best in case someone slides to their knees. If using a driveway or paved area, caution children to be careful when grabbing for the tail. Mark out a circle about 8' in diameter with chalk or rope.

Select two children to begin the game. Tuck an 18" strip of crepe paper or fabric into the back of each child's waistband. Make sure each child's "tail" is the same length. Children stand in the center of the circle, back to back. Ask them to place their hands on their heads. When you announce, "3-2-1, GO!" each child spins around and tries to grab their opponent's tail. Here's where the strategy comes in, because some children try reaching through legs or bending low to the ground. Children must stay within the boundary of the circle and are not allowed to touch the other person except to reach for their tail. Get brave and try playing this against your children. You may have a longer reach, but they'll compensate with lightning-fast speed.

69. Steal the Jewels

Supplies: large flat playing area, small box or can,
metallic spray paint, sequins or costume jewelry, glue
Optional: about forty feet of rope

Games requiring minimum skill are great when working with mixed aged groups. Steal the Jewels gives children of various physical abilities the chance to take part without feeling intimidated by "super-athletes".

Naturally, you'll need a valuable jewel box. Find a small box or can and spray paint it silver or gold. Rather than using your wedding ring or favorite gold necklace, have children glue inexpensive sequins or costume jewelry on the outside and inside of the box to give the impression that the container is filled with priceless jewels.

Designate a large circle about twelve feet in diameter. If you are at the beach or on a dirt field, simply draw a circle on the ground with a stick. On a grassy field, lay a rope down to designate the playing area. Place the jewels in the center of the circle. Everyone stands at the edge of the circle except the "guard," who stands in the center guarding the jewels. On "Go!" children attempt to sneak up to the guard, grab the jewels and get back to outside the circle before being tagged. If they succeed, they change places with the guard and begin keeping watch over the jewels. At first, children will race all at once towards the jewels. This results in the guard easily tagging everyone out. In just a few minutes, strategy develops. Children will pretend to grab the jewels, distracting the guard while another child succeeds in stealing the jewels. Other children try the "sneak-up-behind-and-grab-the-jewels-between-the-guard's-legs" method.

Steal the Jewels is fast-paced, with little emphasis on winning and losing. Adults are at a disadvantage, since they often are not as agile as a typical ten-year-old!

70. Create-a-Game

Supplies: large bags; potential game equipment
such as balls, balloons, boxes, etc.

At gatherings with large groups of children, adults usually
work furiously to plan games. They collect equipment and
carefully explain rules to young players. Instead of doing
all the work yourself, let children create their own games.

Divide children into groups of four to five. Give each
group a bag filled with an assortment of "game" equipment. This could include:

- Various-sized balls
- Frisbees
- Wooden spoons
- Plastic swim noodles
- Balloons
- Hockey sticks
- Empty boxes
- Plastic bottles

Give groups fifteen to twenty minutes to create an
entirely new game using the objects in their bags. Have
adults casually assist each group in the planning process.
After the allocated time, each group explains and demon-
strates their unique game. Then everyone participates in
playing something like "Three-Legged Milk Jug Soccer."

71. So-Small Soccer

Supplies: two shoeboxes, rulers or wooden blocks,
Ping-Pong balls, cardboard paper-towel tubes,
two or more players

Wouldn't it be great to have a full-sized soccer field in your backyard? Then children could run and exercise all day long. If your postage-sized backyard doesn't allow that luxury, make a tabletop soccer field.

Begin with—what else?—a table. That is the playing field. Give children two shoeboxes with the lids removed. Decorate them in black and white or another soccer motif. Set the boxes on each end of the table, with the open sides facing each other, to serve as soccer goals. Use rulers or other long narrow objects taped around the edges of the table to keep the ball from rolling off. Wooden blocks also make great barriers.

After the goals and borders are in place, let the competition begin. Since children don't have room to stand on the table and kick the ball to each end, try a smaller version of soccer. Each child holds an empty cardboard paper-towel tube while standing by opposite ends of the table. Drop a Ping-Pong ball in the center of the playing field. The children blow through the tubes, trying to get their ball into the opposite goal. This means a lot of huffing and puffing. To keep the children from hyperventilating, play only two to three rounds before taking a "breath break."

72. Tabletop Golf

Supplies: 5–8 empty steel cans, golf ball or other
small ball, permanent markers, masking tape,
two or more players

Tiger Woods may be a champion on the professional golf circuit, but your ten-year-old might be the best at tabletop golf. Since this is a game of chance as well as skill, all ages have a fair chance at winning.

Collect five to eight empty cans of various sizes. Make sure that there are no sharp edges around the rim. Wash and dry the cans. If you have extra time, cut construction paper to wrap snugly around each can. Decorate the can with markers or crayons. If golf courses spend thousands of dollars to keep the grass looking nice, you can certainly decorate your tin cans!

Place the cans side by side on a flat surface so that the open edges are lined up. Make tape "doughnuts" by rolling tape sticky-side-out and stick the cans together. Use a permanent marker to write a point value on the inside bottom of each can. Small cans have higher points because it's more difficult to get the ball inside. Large cans might be worth two points compared to a tiny can worth ten points.

Place the connected cans on a table. Stand at the opposite end of the table and try to roll a golf ball or other small ball into a can. Take three turns, add up the score, and let another player take her turn.

73. Crumpled Paper Shoot

Supplies: old newspapers or other scrap paper, tape, wastepaper basket, two or more people

Isn't it pleasant how every evening you can relax in your favorite chair with the newspaper? Your children politely let you read for several hours without interruption. Wake up! It's only a dream. Since you seldom have time to read the paper, go ahead and use it for a game.

Have children crumple up thirty-five to forty sheets of newspaper to make balls. Take several sheets of paper and roll them tightly to make a bat. Tape the edges so it holds its shape. Place a wastepaper basket in the center of the room. Have a child lie on his back, with his head a few inches from the basket, holding the bat. The rest of the family stands on a line, eight to ten feet away, and tries to throw their paper balls into the basket. The laying-down batter attempts to bat them away. Depending on the skill level of the batter, you can throw the newspaper balls one at a time, or fast and furious.

74. Bottle Jug Toss

Supplies: plastic gallon milk jugs, socks, dry beans or rice, permanent markers, sharp scissors

The next time your children clamor for more toys, first tell a heart-wrenching story about your own childhood and your only toy...a rusty tin can. Then help them make their own new game with some household odds and ends.

You'll need several empty plastic milk jugs (thoroughly washed). An adult needs to use sharp scissors and cut off the top third of each jug, leaving the handle part intact. This forms a giant "scoop" for playing catch. Let your children decorate their scoops with permanent markers.

When the scoops are complete, it's time to make the beanbags. You could get out the sewing machine and make square beanbags, or try this simple method. Collect several old socks (without holes). Fill the toe section of each sock with a half cup of dried rice or beans. Tie a knot firmly in the sock and cut off the excess material above the knot. You've just made a durable homemade beanbag.

Have the children hold their scoops by the handle and stand about eight to ten feet from each other. One person slings the beanbag with a scoop while the other person catches it inside his scoop. Try varying the distances between children. Or, instead of beanbags, toss small balls, or water balloons—they may break, but that's all the more fun!

75. Balloon Bat Tennis

Supplies: large flat playing area, wire coat
hangers, panty hose, balloons, scissors
Optional: glue, fabric scraps, yarn

Playing with these homemade tennis "rackets" results in controlled chaos. Children can bat the balloons with little fear of getting hurt or hurting someone else.

Collect wire coat hangers so there is one for each child. Hold the hook end and gently stretch the bottom of the coat hanger so it forms something close to a circular shape. Slip one leg from a pair of panty hose over the metal shape until the foot area is firmly covering your "racket." Cut off excess panty hose. An adult needs to bend the hook together to form a handle. Use duct tape or wide masking tape to attach the cut end of panty hose to the bent handle. This gives a wide, solid batting surface to hit balloons.

Depending on the artistic interest of the group, encourage them to embellish their rackets by setting out an assortment of fabric scraps, yarn, and glue. After the glue dries, you are ready for action.

Blow up several latex balloons or use a mylar balloon that no longer floats. Here are several activities:

○ Toss the balloons in the air and have your children bat them up, trying to keep balloons off the ground.
○ Put up a string or net and let your children bat a balloon back and forth in a modified version of badminton.
○ Have relay races where the children race to a designated finish line, bouncing the balloons off their rackets the entire time.
○ Pair off the children as if participating in an egg toss. Instead of throwing an egg, they try to hit the balloons back and forth to each other.

Silly Games

76. Intricate Chalk Maze

Supplies: sidewalk or driveway, chalk, paper, pencil
Optional: stopwatch

Your children probably have several books filled with intricate mazes. It's fun to put a pencil at the top of a maze and try to reach the exit without being "blocked" or running into a dead end. Enlarge the concept of a maze by drawing one with chalk on your driveway. Then, instead of navigating the maze with a pencil, you navigate it with your whole body.

Drawing a maze is harder than completing a preprinted one. Help your children practice making mazes on paper to understand how to draw one with intricate twists and turns. After they have a general maze design, move out to the driveway. Use the chalk to draw the maze, making sure that the path is wide enough for a person to walk through. Be sure to have a distinct start and finish line.

After everyone in the family has walked through the maze (and hopefully made it to the end) bring out the stopwatch. Time each family member to see who can make the best time beginning at the end and walking backward through the maze to the beginning.

77. Extra-Quick Tic-Tac-Toe

Supplies: sandy beach, sticks, two or more players

Instead of sitting at a table and playing tic-tac-toe with pencil and paper, add excitement by playing in the sand at the beach. To make the game exciting, play close to where the waves come rolling to shore. The goal is to win before the waves erase your game in the sand.

Find an area of the beach where people will not be walking in front of you. Gather two sturdy sticks or use the handles from small shovels to draw in the sand. Draw a tic-tac-toe grid in the sand, near the water's edge. The first person uses his stick to mark an *O* in a block. Quickly, the second player draws an *X* in another block. The game continues until someone wins or the waves come up and wipe out your game board! When that happens, just start all over again.

78. Indoor Obstacle Course

Supplies: household items such as pillows, chairs, sofa cushions, etc.

Sometimes parents resort to drastic measures to keep children occupied during a spell of inclement weather. Forget your traditional furniture arrangements and convert the house (or maybe at least a room) into an indoor obstacle course.

Set ground rules that state how much "construction" is allowed. Can tables be moved, or cushions taken off the couch? (You will probably want to remove breakable objects.) Remind your children that they are responsible for replacing moved items after the game is over. Usually, children are happy for hours just designing the obstacle course, let alone going through it. A few challenges could be:

- Set kitchen chairs in a row so children have to crawl underneath on their stomachs.
- Lay out sofa cushions for a somersaulting section.
- Put a large sheet over a table and crawl underneath.
- Sit on an old towel and scoot on a wood or tile floor, going in and out of boxes.
- Stack pillows in a pile for a "running leap" obstacle.

After the obstacle course is built, time each other to see who can go through in the fastest time. Then watch the children race away as you announce it's time to clean up!

79. Shining Faces

Supplies: flashlights, scissors, paper plates

Every parent loves to see his or her children with bright, smiling faces. When boredom sets in and you find children with grumpy faces, pull out the flashlights. At least they can make artificial smiles.

Give each child a flashlight. (This alone could take awhile as you juggle batteries to get the flashlights to shine.) After the flashlights are in working order, provide several white paper plates for each child. In the center of each plate, cut out faces, jack-o-lantern style. Each plate can have a different face. Try happy, sad, or just plain scary.

Go to a dark room with a plain wall. Hold the paper plate about four or five inches from the wall. With your other hand, shine the flashlight on the plate. The light shines through the cutout pieces, projecting a bright face on the wall. See what happens when you have several shining faces talk to each other. Maybe you'll have an entire choir glowing on the wall, singing "Yellow Submarine."

80. Miniscule Movements

Supplies: none

It's easy to keep children busy with games involving large movements and fast action. Every once in a while, though, children need to keep occupied on a less rowdy level. Try this game where tiny motions are encouraged.

Ask children to move their bodies in funny ways. They can twist or crawl around. When you call out "Miniscule Movements," children freeze in a certain position. They can remain standing or be on the floor. As you walk among the "frozen" bodies, they try to stump you by moving only one tiny part of their body without being detected. Maybe a finger twitches or the very tip of a toe moves. You might have talented children who wiggle their ears. They must keep moving the body part—no fair to stop wiggling their pinkie as you walk by!

Let children take turns being the detective who discovers miniscule movements.

81. Sit Down if You...

Supplies: none

It's often difficult to keep the attention of large groups. Here's a fun way for groups to get to know each other if you are in a confined space.

Ask the group to stand up. If anyone hears a situation that applies to him, he must sit down. Some situations might be:

☺ Sit down if you have a hole in your sock.
☺ Sit down if you cut your own hair when you were little.
☺ Sit down if you sleep with a teddy bear.
☺ Sit down if you have more than two sisters.
☺ Sit down if you like liver.
☺ Sit down if you ever burped in church or temple.
☺ Sit down if you ever tripped over your shoelace.
☺ Sit down if you ever got a 100 on a spelling test.
☺ Sit down if you forgot to brush your teeth today.

Continue playing until everyone sits down. Then start over again with a list of new situations. If you run out of questions, let the group write their own. That saves you work!

82. Noodle Slice Charades

Supplies: plastic swim noodles, cutting board,
sharp knife, paper, pencil

Every family probably has several colorful, long foam noodles used in swimming pools for water play. With a little creativity, noodles provide year-round fun...even on land. They are sold at most discount stores for around two dollars each.

An adult (or older child under supervision) should do the cutting. Lay the long noodle on a hard surface and use a sharp serrated knife to cut it into two-inch slices. (Cutting the dense foam is actually a relaxing, therapeutic process.) It may sound silly, but the slices can provide the basis for many games.

Then, instead of simply playing charades at your next gathering, use the noodle slices to play picture charades. Divide the children into two teams of five to seven kids each. (Make more teams if you have an extra-large group.) Select a team leader from each group and hand them a bag of foam noodle slices. Each team leader also gets a slip of paper with the name of an object on it—both teams get the same word.

On "Go!" the team leaders look at the word and use their noodle slices to "draw" the item while the rest of the team tries to guess the object. One child might depict a lighthouse by making a flat outline, while another stacks the slices on top of each other, making a three-dimensional lighthouse. Children shout out ideas while team leaders frantically try to clarify the picture with more noodle slices. As soon as a team guesses correctly, select another two leaders and give out two more slips of paper with objects. No artistic skill is required!

End the game by having a free-for-all. Let children throw the noodle slices at each other. The foam is so light, no one gets hurt.

Really Goofy Games

83. Crazy Cross The Room

Supplies: large open area

Here's a game that works well with groups ranging from six to sixty people. It's especially fun to include adults, since children enjoy getting to show off their creative ideas.

Line everyone up, shoulder to shoulder, on one side of a room or yard. Designate a "goal" line at least twenty-five feet away. The idea is to have everyone move across the room to the goal line. Here's the catch: select one person and ask them to cross to the line any way they want—except walking. Perhaps that child skips. Anyone else can volunteer to cross, but they can't walk or skip. The next person might twirl, which means the third person can't walk, skip, or twirl. The game continues as each person finds a different, non-repeating way to get to the line. Naturally, if you are the twentieth person to cross, it's difficult to come up with a new idea (especially if you are an adult)!

Children have little difficulty being creative in their movements. You'll see cartwheels, backward crabwalks, and somersaults. Some children get extra-imaginative and pick a partner to cross the room with them. When everyone has crossed to the goal line, the game is over...unless they want to start all over again!

84. The Leader Stands Still

Supplies: none

Anytime you have a group of children, a simple game of Follow the Leader keeps them moving. If you have limited space, here's an adaptation of that familiar game.

Line children up in a row, one behind the other. Leave space between each person for movement. The "leader" is the first child in line. She performs an action such as jumping up and down. The line of children behind her jumps also. Then she waves one arm or wiggles her hips. Children repeat the action. After a few movements, select another child to be leader. After a while it becomes more difficult to think of new movements to do while standing in one place. They could try:

- ◆ Wiggling elbows from side to side
- ◆ Turning in a circle on tippy-toes
- ◆ Bending forward and looking between your legs
- ◆ Doing jumping jacks
- ◆ Attempting to do a sideways split

Children will get creative coming up with ways to twist bodies, lift legs, and wave arms.

85. Moo Baa Quack

Supplies: large, flat playing area

Here's a game that is noncompetitive, suitable for all ages, and lets kids be loud. Sounds like the perfect game, doesn't it?

Gather a large group of children and divide them into two groups. One half are ducks, the others are cows. Put the two halves together and ask children to mingle around, mixing the groups. The game's objective is to find your fellow team members with eyes closed. On "Go!" everyone makes either a cow sound or a duck sound as they slowly walk around the group. Remind children to keep eyes closed. You'll hear a lot of mooing and quacking. When a duck hears another duck, they hold hands and continue walking, searching for another duck. Soon there are four or five ducks or cows walking together. Continue playing until the two sides are completely separated with all the cows together and all the ducks together.

For variation, let children decide on the team categories. You might end up with trains and lions! Try dividing into three or four teams for even louder noise. Bedlam occurs as revving racecars, croaking frogs, chirping crickets, and roaring tigers all search for each other.

Really Goofy Games

86. Tangled-Up Children

Supplies: ball of yarn, four to eight children

Young children playing soccer seem to follow the ball in one mass of bodies. They stay close together, moving as a pack wherever the ball goes. Create your own mass of people by tying a group of children together.

Ask the children to stand close together. Hand one child a ball of yarn. Tie the loose end around his wrist so it doesn't come off. Have the children pass the yarn from person to person, in and out of legs, under arms, and over shoulders. (Have an adult supervise so that no yarn goes around anyone's neck.) Caution children to keep the yarn loose as it connects their bodies.

Once the group is totally tied together, it's time to try to get free! Starting with the last child, they begin rewinding the ball of yarn, untangling and disengaging as the yarn gets passed back to the beginning. This may take a while! Have older children close their eyes during the rewinding process for an extra challenge.

87. Marvelous Moving Machines

Supplies: none

Think about how machines work. All the parts are inter-connected with gears and pulleys working together. Show a group of children how they can be a machine also.

Pick a person to start making a simple machine movement such as raising his arm up and down in the air. Now add a sound, so if the arm is up, he says, "Plink." When the arm comes down, he says, "Kerplop!" Have him continue to do this as another child comes forward and makes her body part of the machine. She might lift her leg as the first person's hand is raised. The second child says, "Chugachoo" each time she lifts her leg. Child number three then comes forward and connects to the machine by creating another element of movement with his body.

One at a time, continue adding people to hook up to the machine. It won't be long until you have a huge machine making all sorts of amazing movements and sounds.

Really Goofy Games

88. Wacky Duck Duck Goose

Supplies: chairs, paper cup or plastic container, water
Optional: confetti, Ping-Pong balls, unpopped popcorn

Duck Duck Goose is a universally popular preschool game. You could spend an hour playing this game at a four-year-old's party with great success. Older children may balk when you suggest playing this game. Dramatically bring out a container of water and you'll catch their attention.

Instead of Duck Duck Goose, you'll be playing Dry, Dry, Wet. The rules are basically the same, except for the added thrill of getting water poured over your head. Have a group of ten to fourteen children sit in a circle. If you have larger groups, make two separate circles. Make sure you are playing in an area where it won't matter if you get wet.

One child is selected to be "It" and walks around the outside of the circle, carrying a cup filled with water. He gently taps people on the head, saying, "Dry, Dry, Dry...WET!" At that point he dumps the water over a sitting child's head. The "wet-head" jumps up and tries to chase "It" around the circle. "It" races to sit down in the empty location before getting tagged. The game continues until everyone has had a chance to get soaked.

Another variation is to prepare a variety of cups ahead of time, filled with assorted items. That way, "It" selects a container and goes around the circle saying, "Not you, not you, not you...it's you!" Then she dumps the cup over the child's head. It could be confetti, Ping-Pong balls, unpopped popcorn, or even the ever-popular cup of water. The suspense increases, as they never know what will land on their heads. One father filled several cups with runny Jell-O, to the delight of everyone.

89. The Nutty Knot

Supplies: none

Children find amazing ways to get shoelaces tied into knots. Then it's a parent's duty to use their front teeth to get the pesky knot untied. Instead of wearing down your teeth, let children tie themselves up in knots in this popular game.

Gather your enthusiastic players and have them form a line, standing side by side. Hold hands. (Not an easy task if working with preteen boys and girls.) Pick the person at one end of the line to be a leader. They begin moving over, under, and around other players, while still holding hands. This results in many contorted bodies. When everyone is smashed together in a tangled mess, begin reversing the movements to untie your human knot. No fair letting go of hands!

Try a slight variation of this game. Stand children side by side in a circle. Have them hold hands with someone who is not standing directly next to them. Get even more tangled by stepping over linked hands or turning backwards. Now try to untie this extra-complicated knot without letting go of hands.

90. Waving Bonnie over the Ocean

Supplies: large sheet or blanket

The perfect tool for this game is a parachute. If you're not a skydiver, bring out the largest sheet you have, which will work just as well. Use a flat sheet, rather than one with fitted corners.

Before playing this game, review the words to "My Bonnie Lies over the Ocean."

My Bonnie lies over the ocean,

My Bonnie lies over the sea,

My Bonnie lies over the ocean.

Oh bring back my Bonnie to me.

Bring back, bring back,

Oh bring back my Bonnie to me, to me.

Bring back, bring back,

Oh bring back my Bonnie to me!

Have children stand around the sheet, holding on to the edges. They'll be tempted to raise it up and down in the air, so let them get it out of their system. Call out directions such as, "Everyone lift the sheet high in the air!" and, "Let's make waves with the sheet!"

When children have settled down, ask them to kneel, holding onto the sheet. As you sing "My Bonnie Lies over the Ocean," they need to alternate standing and kneeling every time they come to a word beginning with *B*. It goes like this:

My Bonnie (stand) lies over the ocean,

My Bonnie (kneel) lies over the sea

Movements get very silly on: Bring (stand) back (kneel) my Bonnie (stand) to me. Bring (kneel) back (stand) etc. This activity also can be performed sitting in chairs instead of kneeling.

91. Gross-Out Sounds

Supplies: body parts!

It's every parent's dream that their precious child would entertain himself by quietly working on multiplication worksheets or discovering a cure for wrinkles. Instead, children will love this game where they get to use their body to make all kinds of disgusting sounds.

It won't take long to get children excited about playing. Begin by asking them to give you samples of sounds they can make. You might get:

- Smacking lips
- Snorts
- Tapping toes
- Clapping hands
- Slapping knees together

After that amazing display of bodily talent, ask one child to be "It" and to turn away. Another child uses his body to make a gross sound. "It" listens and tries to guess the sound. If she guesses correctly, she changes places and a new person is "It." The game continues until all possible body noises have been heard.

92. Strategic Sumo Wrestling

Supplies: pillows, loose T-shirts, two people

If you've suffered through a string of rainy days, even the most conservative parent might resort to Strategic Sumo Wrestling. Some children haven't seen Sumo wrestling on TV, so explain how very large men wrestle each other in fairly slow motion. (No need to model the skimpy loincloth coverings traditional sumo wrestlers wear.)

This activity works with one adult and one child, or two children wrestling each other (under close supervision). Both wrestlers should wear old, loose-fitting shirts because the shirts will never regain their normal shape again. Stuff pillows under the shirts, both in the front and back, for instant Sumo bodies. Tuck the shirt into your pants to keep the pillows secure.

It's time to wrestle! Instead of the fast, jerky movements in traditional wrestling, emphasize that Sumo wrestlers use slow, fluid motions. This also saves wear and tear on your body if you are wrestling with your children.

For the best Sumo wrestling, simply bump into each other's stomachs while emitting loud bursts of obnoxious sounds. (Is it any wonder ten-year-old boys love this activity?) Don't worry about the official rules of Sumo wrestling. You'll have enough fun simply bumping stomachs and then trying to get up as your child pounces on you with his stuffed belly.

Don't forget to take pictures!

93. Furniture Dress-Up

Supplies: socks, shoes, hats, scarves, etc.

Sometimes drastic times call for drastic measures. On those occasions when you've exhausted every game, craft, or activity, it's time to...dress the furniture! Yes, your children will be convinced you've lost a few marbles, but you may get an hour of peace.

Begin a serious discussion with your children on the importance of clothing. (The serious talk leaves them even less prepared for what is to come.) Ask why people wear clothes. What's the purpose of socks? Are coats necessary on a cold day? After a few minutes, announce that you are embarrassed that the furniture in your house is naked. Yes, naked! By now, children are beginning to question your sanity. Keep going. Tell them it is their job to "dress" the furniture.

Try to keep a straight face as you ask children to put shoes on chair legs, socks over doorknobs, and hats on lampshades. In no time at all, children will happily clothe the entire room. Why shouldn't there be a necklace draped over the back of a chair or scarves tied jauntily around a vase?

One mother, obviously *very* desperate for an activity, brought down the dirty clothes hamper and dumped it on the floor. "Here," she announced. "Use these clothes to get the family room decently dressed." After the room was modestly covered with socks and shirts, she took pictures and then everyone carried the dirty laundry directly to the washing machine.

Really Goofy Games

94. Super Sock Grab

Supplies: One child, one adult, two socks

Never—repeat, never—try this activity right before bed-time. The excitement and energy level will have your child (and you) up long past midnight. The premise is simple: try to remove the sock from your opponent's foot before they grab your sock.

It may be its simplicity that accounts for the popularity of this game. For best results, play on a bed, the bigger the better. If you have a California King bed, you're on pre-miere playing ground.

Each player wears one sock, slipped over the top half of his or her foot. (It doesn't cover the heel of the foot.) Kneel in the middle of the bed, facing your child. Clap three times to signal the start of the round. Try to grab the sock from your child's foot while they are attempting to grab your sock. Usually this means that you are on your hands and knees on a soft bed, with one leg straight out behind you. Naturally, this leaves you vulnerable to being thrown off balance by your younger, more agile son or daughter. Whoever grabs a sock first is the winner. Don't think your child will be satisfied with just one round. This game lasts until the adult runs out of breath and admits defeat.

Don't forget to remove any breakable or valuable items from nightstands. This game can be played on the floor, but being on a bed increases the fun because of the additional risk of falling off.

95. Meet the Tricky Trickster

Supplies: plastic ants, ice cube trays, food coloring, salt, embroidery floss

Ever feel like all you do is nag your children? Wonder if you've lost your sense of humor? Think you should "lighten up"? Simply follow a few of these ideas and your children will be wondering what comedy class you attended.

It doesn't take much to bring a lighthearted atmosphere to your family. In some homes, just saying "dirty diapers" sets children off on a giggling fit. Go to the library and get some books with tricks, jokes, and riddles. Start out by telling a joke at dinner. Don't worry if you can't remember the punch line. Children will laugh at your memory loss. Try these ideas also:

- Purchase tiny plastic ants and put them in an ice cube tray. Add water, freeze, and serve the ice cubes in drinks to your unsuspecting family.
- Add green food coloring to scrambled eggs and read *Green Eggs and Ham* at breakfast to your children.
- Challenge a family member by saying, "Chrysanthemum. Can you spell it?" As they blunder through the spelling, proudly announce, "I said spell IT. I-T!" This is definitely elementary school humor.
- Give each member a bowl with ice cubes. (Frozen ants are optional.) Ask them to try and lasso the ice cube with a twelve-inch piece of embroidery floss. After they give up in frustration, bring out the saltshaker. Lay the thread on top of an ice cube and sprinkle a generous helping of salt on top. Wait thirty seconds for the thread to melt into the ice. With a grand flourish, lift up

the loose end of the thread to show off your incredible ability to lasso an ice cube.

That's just the beginning. Once you see how easy it is to add fun to your family, you'll be performing magic tricks and juggling bowling balls.

Wordplay

96. All about Me

Supplies: paper, pencil

Children frequently have acrostic worksheets to do in school. Instead of filling in the blanks on a preprinted piece of paper, encourage them to make up an acrostic describing themselves.

Give children paper and pencil. Demonstrate how to write their name, one letter at a time, from the top to the bottom of the page. Then write descriptions about them that begin with each letter in their name. Example: SEAN

S: swims very fast

E: eats raw broccoli

A: always is kind to the dog

N: needs a raise in allowance!

After everyone makes an acrostic for their own name, switch names. Give children the name of someone else in the family to describe in the form of an acrostic.

Wordplay

97. Make a List

Supplies: paper, pencil

Did you ever get to the grocery store and realize you've for-gotten your shopping list? What happens if you lose your "to-do" list? Yes, lists are important to us. Teach children how to make lists of their own in this easy activity.

Everyone needs a pencil and paper. Younger children can make verbal lists. Present a subject and ask children to list as many items as possible under that category. Examples could be:

- List things a dog likes to eat.
- List things Dad likes to eat!
- List items needed if you're going on a camping trip.
- List ways to travel around the world.
- List things that make noise if you bang them together.
- List items that break when dropped.
- List people who have given you a present.
- List ideas for a new flavor of ice cream.

After everyone finishes writing their lists, take turns sharing the results.

98. Name Game

Supplies: paper, pencils, three or more players

Salespeople know the importance of using a customer's name to build rapport. This game lets everyone have fun creating words from their own name.

Provide paper and pencils for everyone. Pick one child to be the "star." Everyone writes that child's first and last name on his or her paper. Then, in five minutes, they try to come up with as many words as possible using the letters in the child's name. If the children are older, increase the challenge by specifying that the words have to be at least three letters long.

At the end of the time period, read off the lists and determine a winner based on best word, longest word, or longest list. The winner's grand prize? A hug from the "star" child! Continue playing until all family members have had their name used.

99. Telephone Number Jingles

Supplies: paper, pencil

Ask someone their phone number and they'll easily rattle off the seven-digit number. Yet more and more companies incorporate the letters connected to each number on the telephone keypad. It's easy to remember 1-800-FLOWERS. Keep older children occupied by having them make up words connected with phone numbers.

A small amount of preparation is required. Simply sketch out the twelve boxes of a telephone keypad. Draw three squares across and four squares down. Write down each number and the corresponding three letters. For example, box 2 includes *A*, *B*, and *C*, and box 3 includes *D*, *E*, and *F*. Give each child a copy of your artistic rendition of a telephone keypad.

Give children a telephone number and ask them to list any words that can be formed from the letters. If you give them 744-6673, someone is sure to come up with "Pig-Nose." Now that's a great phone number!

100. Alphabet Antics

Supplies: none

Word games are popular with children because they can display their years of accumulated knowledge. Alphabet Antics requires concentration (which usually lowers the noise level).

Select a broad category such as "animals" or "people." The first person names an item from that category, such as the ever-popular "dog." The next person must think of an animal that starts with "G", the last letter of the stated word. It might go like this:

☺ DoG
☺ GoaT
☺ Tabby caT
☺ TigeR
☺ RhinoceroS
☺ Snake

Keep going until you run out of animals. An animal can't be repeated. Younger children might need you to tell them what letter to use. For older children, use narrower categories like "Flowers" or "States." They'll have to think when the word sequence goes like this:

☺ DandelioN
☺ NasturtiuM
☺ MarigolD
☺ DaisY
☺ Yellow daffodil

Wordplay

101. See It But Don't Say It

Supplies: six to eight household items like shoes, books, keys, coins, etc.; five or more people

It takes extra coordination to have one hand do one movement while the other hand attempts a different movement. Ask your children to try and write their names on a piece of paper while making a circular motion with their feet—the two actions are difficult to do at the same time. Now play a game where you have to concentrate on naming an object that is *not* in your hand.

The group sits in a circle, close enough to pass around an item. Collect six to eight items such as a shoe, banana, penny, etc. Hand one person an object such as a book. Since book starts with the letter *B*, they hold the book and say the name of something else that starts with *B*. They might say "boxes," and pass the book to the next person. The game continues with each person holding the book and naming another object. It's difficult to have a book in your hand and say "birdhouse."

Continue playing until someone can't think of a word with *B*. Pass out another object such as a fork and begin the process using words beginning with *F*. If playing with older children, select an adult to clap out a certain beat to keep the objects moving quickly around the circle.

102. Show Me the Cash

Supplies: paper, pencils

Anytime you deal with money, children suddenly become interested. This activity helps improve children's math skills without them knowing you're playing an educational game.

Make up a chart listing the letters of the alphabet. Assign each letter a random amount of money, such as A = $2.00, B = 25¢, etc. Hand your child the chart and start the math process.

Ask your child what the dog's name would add up to. This encourages your child to add up the numbers connected with the letters F-r-i-s-k-y. Continue the challenge by asking, "If I gave you $50.00, what word could I buy?" "What long word would add up to $675.00?"

Just be thankful you don't have to pay your child for spelling every word on her spelling list!

Wordplay

103. Detailed Descriptions

Supplies: none

Children forget to put their dirty clothes in the hamper, but can remember with vivid detail the last video they saw. Use their powers of memory and observation by playing this game.

Pick a child and say, "Emily, please tell us ten things you would find at the dentist's office." After she lists ten, ask other family members if they can think of additional things. Give each family member a location and have him or her recall items found there. Possible places are:

◆ A beauty shop
◆ The library
◆ The skating rink
◆ Grandma's attic
◆ A golf course
◆ Inside an ambulance
◆ A gymnastic center
◆ A bakery
◆ Inside the trunk of the car
◆ A school bus
◆ A clown's suitcase

Instant Fun

104. Fun in a Flash

Supplies: various household items

You have an extra few minutes before dinner. The dentist is late and you need to wait ten more minutes. When you suddenly need to pass the time together, here are some tried and true favorites you can do on the spur of the moment.

- Make a chain out of paper clips.
- Juggle pillows or whatever is around you.
- Read a book together.
- Start working on a puzzle.
- Find a strange word in the dictionary and make up a definition.
- See how high you can stack plastic cups.
- Use a tape measure to measure people, doors, and your car.
- Teach the dog a new trick.
- Have a spelling bee.
- Write words on a person's back with your finger.
- Tell knock-knock jokes.
- Practice a fire-safety drill.
- Build a house out of cards.
- See whose paper airplane flies the farthest.

Instant Fun

105. Crazy Categories

Supplies: none

Most children like being part of a group. It's comforting to wear the same general style of clothes and listen to the same music. Here's a way for children to categorize themselves into a variety of groups.

Explain to the children that you'll be announcing different categories ranging from hair color to number of freckles. Their job is to line themselves up side by side in the order you describe. Try some of these criteria:

- from shortest to tallest
- in order of birthday months (January, February etc.)
- by the color of your socks, from darkest to lightest
- according to number of freckles
- by the number of buttons on your clothing

With older children, make the game harder by having them line up without talking. You'll see some creative communication take place.

106. Crazy Coin Flip

Supplies: coin

Most children resist going on walks under the guise of being bored. Add some mystery to an ordinary walk by letting a coin determine where you'll end up.

For best results, you'll need to be in an area that has numerous cross streets or a park with many intersecting trails.

Begin by having a child toss a coin. "Heads" means you'll turn left. "Tails" means you're headed to the right. Walk in the direction indicated by the coin until the next cross street or trail. Again, flip the coin to see which direction you'll go. You might be surprised where you end up. Let the children take turns flipping the coin at each intersection. (This is also a great way to teach your children their right from their left.) Watch what happens when you are standing on a street corner and a left turn would lead you to an ice cream shop...and the coin tells you to go right!

As you walk, take time to explore. Point out various styles of architecture or try to remember high school biology and identify plants. Some families find themselves far away from their starting point, and have to forget flipping the coin on the way home or they'd be out until midnight. Make sure you don't get lost.

Instant Fun

107. Chain-Link Fence Weaving

Supplies: chain-link fence, rolls of crepe paper or plastic surveyor's tape (available inexpensively at hardware stores)

Ever had one of those days where nothing you do seems to stop your children from bickering or complaining? It may sound strange, but children find it therapeutically calming to weave streamers in and out of a chain-link fence. (It helps to have a chain-link fence nearby.)

Announce, "Your job is to weave a design in the backyard fence." Disregard the strange looks your children give you. Hand them rolls of crepe paper streamers or, better yet, plastic surveyor's tape. Surveyors use these rolls of thin plastic to mark boundaries. Rolls cost less than a dollar at hardware stores and come in many bright colors. Let your children decide how to create patterns by weaving in and out of the fence.

Some children get so enthusiastic, they figure out how to weave their name among the fence links. Other children make multicolor-striped designs. Many day camps keep this activity going as a summer-long project. Children need little supervision while they weave, and it can keep them happily occupied for hours. Feel free to join in!

108. Balancing Brooms

Supplies: rulers, yardsticks, brooms

Baby boomers remember *The Ed Sullivan Show* featuring a man who balanced poles on his hands and feet while plates twirled overhead. We all held our breath, wondering how he could keep so many plates spinning at once.

To save your good china, I don't recommend that children try to spin plates on top of poles. You can, however, have fun trying to balance poles and other items on your hands and feet. Begin by attempting to balance a ruler upright in the palm of your hand. No fair grabbing it with fingers! Gently cup your hand and try to move around with the ruler standing straight up. Make sure the area is free from rocks or toys. Children get so focused on balancing their object that they don't see that football on the ground.

After children master balancing a ruler, move on to bigger and better things. Get plenty of room and try to balance a yardstick or broom handle while slowly moving back and forth. If you have super balancers, challenge them to stand on one foot and balance the broom on top of their toes. If the guy on *Ed Sullivan* can do it, your ten-year-old can!

109. Funny Funnel Trick

Supplies: large funnel, quarter

Games of skill are a big hit with children. Playing the funny funnel trick is a chance to demonstrate physical coordination or, with adult approval, an innocent practical joke.

Find a funnel, the bigger the better. If you're using one from the garage, clean off the oil and grease. Get a volunteer to stick the pointed end of the funnel in the front of his pants so it sits securely. Ask the volunteer to tip his head back so you can place a quarter on his forehead. This results in a comical body position, since he has to stick his stomach out to keep the funnel in his pants while balancing the quarter on his forehead. The objective is for the volunteers to lean their heads forward and try to drop the quarter into the funnel. Usually it takes several attempts to get the quarter to land where it should. Let everyone try and then have a contest to see who can get the quarter in the funnel the most times consecutively.

This activity can easily be turned into a practical joke if you feel it's appropriate. While a person stands with the funnel in their pants and their head tipped back with a quarter on it, quickly pour a glass of water down the funnel! This is a huge hit with ten-year-old boys.

110. Eight-Armed Dressing

Supplies: large T-shirt

Getting children dressed in the morning becomes a major battle in some homes. Parents constantly admonish, "Hurry up, you'll be late for school!" Perhaps playing this game will help children appreciate how easy it is to get dressed on their own.

Gather children into groups of four. Hand each group a very large T-shirt. The shirt is likely to get stretched out, so make sure it is not your favorite. Put the shirt over one child's regular clothing. Have the group all hold hands. Here's where creative thinking takes place. Tell the group they need to take the shirt off of their team member and put it on any other person in their group. Sounds easy doesn't it? The only catch is they must keep holding hands the entire time!

It takes fancy maneuvering and cooperation to get the shirt transferred to another person. Suggest to children that they tuck their own shirts securely into their pants before playing this game. Otherwise they may literally lose their shirts when transferring the baggy T-shirt. The next time your children seem slow getting dressed, tell them how lucky they are not to be attached to three others.

Instant Fun

111. Shaky Shadow Shows

Supplies: bright light, plain wall

Children always delight in watching slides projected on the wall. It is even more fun to hold your hand in front of the projector and make goofy shadows with your hands. If you can't find a slide projector, use a bright light and teach your children how to make "bunny ears" on the wall.

Select a room with one white, blank wall. A large, solid-colored sheet thumbtacked to the wall also works. On the other side of the room, place a bright light such as a flood-light or a lamp without a shade. Show your child how to stand a few feet from the wall and project her shadow on the wall. Instead of just using hands for shadows, see what shapes you can make with your whole body.

Experiment with shadow sizes. The closer you are to the wall, the smaller the shadow becomes. Step toward the light, and the shadow becomes larger. Have two children stand close together, forming one body shadow. If they spread their heads apart, the shadow looks like a two-headed monster.

112. Count the Change

Supplies: coins, two or more people

As dutiful parents, we help our children with the basics of addition and subtraction. We try to make flashcards interesting, but sometimes nothing works except cold hard cash. Here's a way to truly motivate your children to learn how to add or subtract.

Find an open area like the center of the living room. Since children will be "diving," remove all breakable items from the vicinity. Better yet, go outside to a grassy area.

Hold a handful of change. Stand the children in a line, a few feet away from you. Toss ten to twelve coins on the ground and yell out, "Twenty-two cents!" Children race to the coins, trying to add them up to reach twenty-two cents. Older children can get creative and bring you a quarter and three pennies, saying, "Twenty-five minus three equals twenty-two." And they are correct!

Continue playing several rounds. Occasionally announce, "Whoever gets the next round correct gets to keep the change!" You'll see children quickly learning their math facts. With older children, throw out more change and give multiplication challenges.

Instant Fun

113. Drop Off!

Supplies: table, small unbreakable item

Have you ever sat at a restaurant with hungry children? You know the agony of waiting for the meal to finally arrive and fill their hungry stomachs. Pass the time by playing a daredevil game of Drop Off!

Sit at a smooth table, across from each other. Select a small unbreakable item to serve as the game piece. In restaurants, sugar packets work well.

Person No. 1 scoots the object across the table, trying to get it as close to the edge as possible. It takes practice to get the right amount of "slide" so the object doesn't fall off the edge. At first, you might give a gentle push and find that the object doesn't even reach the mid-point. Take turns sliding items as close to the edge as possible. Some people keep score for who gets closest to the edge, but it's not necessary. Try playing this on a picnic table on a sunny day. Instead of using sugar packets, use paper cups filled with water. Suddenly, the tension increases!

114. Funny Foil Friends

Supplies: aluminum foil, pipe cleaners

When looking for activities to keep children occupied on car or plane trips, the first consideration is usually, "Is this a quiet activity?" You'll be pleasantly surprised at just how quiet children can be as they work to create amazing foil sculptures. We're so busy wrapping sandwiches in foil, we neglect the possibilities of tiny silver people.

The only two supplies needed are pieces of foil and some pipe cleaners. Provide children with several sheets of foil in various sizes. Give some basic guidance such as, "Why don't we start by making foil figures of ourselves?" Children easily (and quietly) mold and shape the foil. It's easy to incorporate the pipe cleaners for arms and legs or even halos. Wrap the foil around pipe cleaners for moveable silver joints. Foil tears easily, so children can make any size they want.

It won't be long until you have amassed a collection of people, animals, and space creatures. By now you're probably thinking, "Why haven't I given my children foil before?"

Instant Fun

115. What's Different?

Supplies: none

Some children are very detail-oriented, noticing every new gray hair on your head (and never hesitating to point it out to you). Check their powers of observation by playing this low-key game.

Select one person to be the "spy." It's the spy's job to have a keen eye for subtle differences in the other family members' appearances. Have everyone stand in front of the spy and slowly turn around. This gives the spy a chance to thoroughly see what each family member is wearing, how they have their hair, etc.

Ask the spy to leave the room. When the coast is clear, the remaining players change five things about their appearance. Possibilities include:

- ✪ Button or unbutton one button.
- ✪ Change the part in your hair.
- ✪ Tuck your shirt in if it was hanging out of your pants, or pull it out if it was tucked in.
- ✪ Scrunch down your socks.
- ✪ Tie a double knot in your shoelace.
- ✪ Put your watch on the opposite wrist.

When the spy returns, his job is to find the changes in each person's appearance. At first, the differences are obvious, but after several rounds of play, you'll find family members getting very clever at doing subtle changes. Make things more interesting by switching socks or hair clips with family members. This makes the spy's job even more complicated.

116. Modified William Tell

Supplies: brave child, soft ball or piece of foam, apple

Remember the story of William Tell? He was a famous archer in Switzerland during the 1700s. Due to a confrontation with the king, he was forced to shoot an apple off the head of his twelve-year-old son, Walter. Would you be brave enough to shoot an arrow anywhere even close to your son? Instead of finding an archery set, try this safe version of the William Tell game.

Read your children the story of William Tell, or tell it in a modified version. Have your child stand against a wall and balance an apple on his head. (This could take a while.) When the apple has stopped wobbling, use a soft object like a wadded-up tissue ball and throw it at the apple. See how much your child trusts you!

For more fun, reverse roles and have your children try to hit the apple on your head. It's a good thing you're not using real arrows.

Instant Fun

117. Guess That Shape

Supplies: pencil, household items, unlined paper

Sometimes the easiest, most low-tech activities keep children occupied the longest. Turn children loose with paper and pencil for a tracing experience that helps everyone see ordinary objects in a new light.

Give each child several pieces of plain, unlined paper along with pencils or markers. Bring out a few household items such as a potholder or a stuffed animal. Show your children how to place the paper on a flat surface, set an item on top, and trace around the object. Often, the traced figure is difficult to recognize. (Would you be able to recognize the tracing of a partially chewed dog's rawhide bone?)

Set an allocated amount of time to return from tracing objects, in and out of the house. When everyone returns with his or her drawings, try to guess each item. Some will be obvious, while others are barely recognizable.

If you like, pick two or three items and try to incorporate them into a picture. The tracing of a fork could be the body of a thin, scared person, with hair standing on end. A tracing of a shoe might serve as the basis of a new form of dinosaur.

118. Creative Answering-
Machine Message

Supplies: answering machine

If a survey were taken, the results would show that ninety-eight out of every one hundred answering machine messages say, "Sorry we can't come to the phone right now. Leave a message at the beep and we'll call you back." Give your children free rein (within the limits of good taste) to create their own outgoing message for the answering machine.

Ask them to jot down various scripts and practice without the machine. Try saying something like, "If you are a salesperson, please leave your message *before* the beep." After three or four scripts, your children will get silly and be reduced to giggles as they attempt another unique message. Let them go. Eventually they'll come up with something clever and useful.

Here are a few suggestions:

☺ Take a popular show tune and change the words to fit the message.
☺ Have two children do a short dialogue back and forth.
☺ Come up with a short poem that tells people to leave their number.

After children practice their messages, have a family vote to decide on the actual recording. Then all that's left is trying to get the message on the machine without your children succumbing to a fit of giggles.

Instant Fun

Scavenger Hunts

119. Fantasy Scavenger Hunt

Supplies: paper, pencil, collection boxes or bags, assorted household items

There's something so exciting about going on a scavenger hunt. Children love the thrill of locating an item and then racing to be the first team to collect all their items. A fantasy scavenger hunt provides excitement while encouraging children to be creative. Announce ahead of time that this game has no winners or losers. Sometimes the hardest part of this activity is for adults to come up with the imaginative items required on the search list.

Before the event begins, make a list of ten to twelve "fantasy" items. You will need a copy of the list for each team. Items could include:

◆ A bed for fairies
◆ A new type of "sorting" hat for Harry Potter to use at Hogwarts
◆ A cooking utensil you could use if you were eating underwater
◆ Something to massage your scalp if you are bald
◆ An item to use for taking your pet dinosaur on a walk
◆ A new piece of exercise equipment

Divide the group into teams of two or three children, giving each team the same list of items to find. Provide each team with a box or bag to collect their treasures. Designate fifteen to twenty-five minutes for the teams to find or make each object on the list...plus come up with an explanation of how it fulfills the requirements. For example, one group might bring a garden hose and explain how they would tie it around the neck of a dinosaur and use it as an extra-long leash. Half the fun is listening to each team describe why they chose the item they did.

120. Evening Treasure Hunts

Supplies: flashlights, assortment of toys and small items

Even in the summer, children seldom get the chance to spend time outdoors at night. They may come home from the mall when it's dark, but then quickly walk from the car into the house. If you live in an area with a fenced backyard, try an evening treasure hunt.

Don't worry if you don't have pots of gold to hide. Children are happy searching for stuffed animals, action figures, or even peanuts in the shell. Some parents hide gold foil–covered chocolate coins and say they are pirate coins. Another option is to hide treats in plastic Easter eggs; the eggs can be used year-round.

Hide whatever objects you have throughout the backyard. Try to keep most of the objects in plain view since children will be searching with flashlights. When it finally gets dark and you can't contain the children any more, set them loose with a bag to stash their loot. Turn out most of the house lights so the yard is dark. Children will race through the yard, shining flashlights along fence posts and in tree branches. It's a magical experience to be outside in the dark, searching for treasure.

121. Wild Animal Hunt

Supplies: stuffed animals, large box

While it would be nice to head off on an African safari to see wild animals living in their natural habitat, you might have to settle for stuffed animals in your cluttered living room. This activity works well when children need to move around, yet it still avoids total bedlam.

Begin by asking your children to bring you all of their stuffed animals. If you have Beanie Baby collectors, their collection alone is all you need. Place the stuffed menagerie in a box (or several boxes). Have the children wait in a bathroom or outside the front door so you have free rein of the house. As soon as the children are sequestered, take your box of stuffed toys and hide them throughout the house. Depending on the age of your children, stuffed animals can be in plain view or hidden under a pile of laundry.

When the toys are hidden, explain the main rule to children: if they open drawers, move books, etc., they must return the item the way they found it. This avoids children leaving a trail of upturned furniture looking for stuffed animals. Make a big production of announcing the beginning of the hunt and let them go.

As they collect the stuffed toys, they'll get plenty of exercise moving throughout the house. After the last toy is found, let another child hide them all over again. After all, it's the thrill of the hunt!

122. Nature Scavenger Hunt

Supplies: paper, pencil, collection boxes or bags, outdoor area

Scavenger hunts give children the opportunity to work together as a team while running frantically from one location to another. With a nature scavenger hunt, they'll also (hopefully) develop an awareness of their environment.

Before the event, make a list of ten to twelve natural items. You will need a copy of the list for each team. Items could include:

- A twig or branch in the shape of the letter *Y*
- A bird feather
- A piece of tree bark that fell to the ground
- The biggest leaf you can find
- The smallest leaf you can find
- A rock in the shape of a heart
- Five pinecones
- A piece of moss

Divide the group into teams of three or four children, giving each team a collection box or bag and a list of items to find. Stress the importance of collecting only leaves and plants on the ground and being careful not to trample any vegetation. Announce the time allowed and let them take off! The winner is the first team returning with all the correct items. Some groups enjoy simply racing to get their list completed and don't even care about designating a "winner."

123. Dinosaur Egg Scavenger Hunt

Supplies: watermelon, paper, pencils, aluminum foil or spray paint

Gather a group of children together. With a look of total amazement, explain that a dinosaur has left a giant egg hidden in the area. If you have skeptics, make up an official dinosaur-sounding name like "Tranperdotious Puglexia." Now they'll believe you!

Ahead of time, buy a dinosaur egg at the grocery store. Actually, you'll simply spray paint a watermelon silver, or wrap it in aluminum foil. Hide the "egg" in a discreet location.

Hand children a piece of paper with a clue to the dinosaur egg's location. If you are really clever, put the clues in rhyme, such as:

Be careful, you might need a guide

As you slip down the plastic _____.

At the end of the slide would be a clue leading to the next location. Make up as many clues as you can think of. This keeps children running from one location to another, burning off energy. The last clue should lead them to the dinosaur egg. One energetic mother dug a hole and buried the egg to add to the authenticity of the dinosaur egg hunt. As you slice the watermelon, remind children that the seeds are actually tiny dinosaur eggs.

124. Taking Inventory

Supplies: paper, pencils

Each January, stores hire extra staff to count items for an accurate inventory of their merchandise. Send children on a mission to inventory items in your home. It might be an eye-opening experience to see how many material things your family has accumulated.

Make an official-looking tabulation inventory sheet for each child. List items such as:

- Number of toothbrushes in the house
- Mom's shoes
- Hammers
- Tires on cars (don't forget the spare tire in the trunk)
- Cans of vegetables
- Bricks around the fireplace
- Books
- Potholders
- Towels
- Wastebaskets
- Pictures on the walls
- Dolls
- Stuffed animals
- Lego pieces

After the children have counted and recorded the numbers on their sheets, share the information. Compare how many books you *think* you have with the actual count. All these items might inspire you to have a garage sale and reduce your personal inventory!

125. Guess That Sound!

Supplies: tape recorder and tapes

Many parents remember the thrill of working a reel-to-reel tape recorder back in the stone ages. Years later we moved on to high-tech cassette tape recorders. Even though your children are familiar with DVDs and computers, they'll still enjoy collecting sounds on a good old-fashioned tape recorder.

If you can't find a portable tape recorder in a closet, check a neighborhood garage sale. People will gladly take your dollar to get rid of their unwanted recorder. Show children how to operate the machine. Then turn them loose in the house and yard on a "sound hunt," recording ten to fifteen seconds of ordinary, everyday sounds. Tell them you'll try and guess the sounds. These could include:

- Toilet flushing
- Cat meowing
- Dishwasher running
- Video ejecting from the machine
- Brothers and sisters fighting!
- Someone gargling
- Wind blowing through the trees
- Car horn honking
- Dad singing in the shower
- Door slamming

After the recording is complete, listen to the recording and try to guess each sound. Keep the recorder handy to record bits of sounds such as "Claire practicing the piano" or "Michael bouncing a basketball in the driveway." When friends or relatives visit, play the tape and see if they can guess the source of the sounds.

126. Museum Postcard Scavenger Hunt

Supplies: postcards

Deep inside every parent lies the urge to "do something educational" for their children. That's why late at night we look up answers to such questions as, "How do the clouds get their funny shapes?" and, "If gravity pulls things down, how come I can stand on my head and eat a banana?" Then we take our children to an art museum in order to instill a sense of culture in their lives.

With so many hands-on children's museums available, children are used to poking and exploring every display in a museum. It comes as a shock when they enter an "adult" museum and are told, "Don't touch!" Use a series of post-cards to help children feel a part of the museum experience (and get some educational value out of the tour also).

As you enter the museum, explain the difference between an art gallery, complete with guards at valuable paintings, and the controlled chaos at the local children's museum. Children behave better knowing the situation in advance. Make your first stop a visit to the gift shop. Purchase six to eight postcards depicting paintings or exhibits inside the museum. Take time to read the short description on the back of the postcards.

Help your children look for the actual painting or exhibit on the postcard. They can ask a museum curator, wander aimlessly, or check a museum directory. In any case, they are actively involved in researching the museum. Keep the first museum visits short. Match the postcards to several paintings and leave on an upbeat note. Your child's first memory of an art museum will be positive and soon you'll be ready to search out the Mona Lisa at the Louvre.

127. Airport Scavenger Hunt

Supplies: paper, pencil

It's every parent's nightmare. Those dreaded words come over the microphone: "Flight 438 will have a two-hour delay." Naturally you are on flight 438. Instead of grumbling, decide to go on an airport scavenger hunt. You will need two adults in order to carry out this activity.

Have one adult stay with the children while you prepare your scavenger list. Walk through the airport with paper and pencil. Write down items for children to locate such as:

- ☺ A handicapped accessible restroom
- ☺ A store selling pretzels
- ☺ An information booth
- ☺ A view of the airport control tower
- ☺ Rental cars
- ☺ An espresso stand
- ☺ A place to get a massage
- ☺ Airport gift shop

Return to your children (make sure you can remember where they are). Give them the list and see if they can find the items on the list. This can be a group effort, or turn it into friendly competition. Quickly write the list a second time. Divide the group in half and have an adult go with each team. The first one back with all the items checked off is declared the winning team.

Playing
with Your
Food

128. Elaborate Egg Drop

Supplies: second-story window, eggs,
boxes, cushioning materials

Many high school students are assigned this activity during science classes. Give your children a head start into higher education by working with them on making a device that keeps an egg from breaking.

Decide in advance if this is a joint family effort or each man (or woman) for himself. Some families give each child a raw egg and let them work on their own. In any event, the goal is to build a container that protects an egg when dropped from a second-story window. If you don't have a second floor, just go to a neighbor's house and say, "Hi, George. The family and I would like to traipse through your house and drop some eggs out your bedroom window. Thanks."

Set a time limit of thirty to forty-five minutes to build the container. Let the kids search for boxes, padding, and anything else they can find to provide a soft and safe drop-container. Try to avoid giving too much guidance. The experimentation process is important for your children.

After the contraptions are built and the eggs are snug inside, let each family member carefully throw their own egg out the second-story window. Try not to knock each other over as you all race downstairs to see if your egg survived. Make a big production out of opening each container to see if there is a solid egg inside or a slimy mess.

129. Blindfolded Banana Guess

Supplies: assorted cut-up fruits and vegetables,
scarf or bandana for blindfold
Optional: various brands of cola

"I like potatoes better the way Grandma makes them."

"These peas taste mushy. I like firm peas."

Do your children have distinct taste preferences? See if their taste buds are really as sensitive as they claim them to be.

With your children in another room, set out a variety of bite-sized pieces of food. Cut up fruit, or put out dollops of yogurt and sour cream. For added mystery, slice a few pieces of raw potatoes and onion also. Cover the food with a clean cloth so peeking eyes can't see the items.

Invite the rest of the family into the room and ask for volunteers willing to be blindfolded to try and guess what food you are serving. As soon as a brave soul steps up, put a dark scarf around her eyes. Hand her a food item and see if she can guess what it is by taste alone. Surprisingly, many picky eaters have trouble identifying foods when they can't be seen. Ask your volunteer to remain blindfolded and pinch her nose while she is tasting the food. The sense of smell often helps us identify foods. With sight and smelling blocked, an onion ends up tasting like an apple.

For an adaptation on this activity, purchase three brands of cola. Let family members taste each brand and try to identify them.

130. Dancing Raisins

Supplies: glasses, raisins, carbonated
water or club soda

If you don't have the energy to dance the night away, at least help your children enjoy a glass of dancing raisins.

Begin with a clear glass or jar filled with at least one cup of carbonated water or club soda. Drop in several raisins and watch what happens. The raisins (if they're in a dancing mood) should rise up and down in the glass.

The carbonation in the water collects on the bumpy raisin edges. After enough carbon dioxide gas collects, it "propels" the raisin to the water surface. The gas releases into the air and the raisin sinks. Then the dancing begins all over again. Some people report success in getting raisins to dance by using 7-Up or Sprite.

For a wilder dance party, drop two Alka Seltzer tablets into a cup of water. Watch how the raisins begin jitterbugging! What happens if children add grapes or cherry tomatoes? You might have an entire dancing garden.

131. Crunchy Colored Pasta

Supplies: uncooked pasta, bowls, rubbing alcohol,
food coloring, old newspaper

Craft stores sell expensive bags of brightly colored pasta in various shapes so children can decorate cans or embellish pictures with blue and yellow pasta. "Ahhh," you think. "I could just put pasta into some colored water and dye it myself." Guess what happens? The pasta gets dyed all right, but it also turns mushy.

Here's the secret art teachers don't want you to know: water makes pasta soft, but rubbing alcohol keeps pasta firm. Set out several small bowls and pour two or three tablespoons of rubbing alcohol in each. (If you have young children, caution them about getting drops of alcohol on their hands and then touching their eyes.) Add a few drops of food coloring to each bowl. Gently drop in several tablespoons of various pasta shapes and stir. It only takes a few minutes for the dyed alcohol to be absorbed into the pasta. Remove the pasta with a slotted spoon and let it dry overnight on old newspaper. The next day you'll have hard, brightly colored pasta. Try stringing them on yarn for a one-of-a-kind necklace, or glue on paper to make colorful designs.

132. Frozen Hot Dog Weaving

Supplies: frozen washcloths, rubber bands, balls of yarn or string

Okay, your children aren't really going to weave with hot dogs. They will get a kick out of weaving a frozen rolled-up washcloth in and out of their clothes. The traditional way of playing this game is to tie a spoon to the end of a ball of yarn. Why use an ordinary spoon when you could add an element of ice?

At least a day before the big event, wet several washcloths and roll them up tightly. Wrap several rubber bands around to help keep the tube shape (hence the name "hot dog"). When it's time to play, remove the frozen washcloths and tie the end of a ball of yarn to each one. Line up children into three or four even lines, relay race style. The first child in each line passes the frozen "hot dog" down from the neck of their shirt (next to their skin) and out from the bottom of their shirt. They then pass the frozen washcloth to the next person in line who repeats the process. Pretty soon the whole line is woven together, connected by the yarn.

Once the last person has completed the task, reverse the process so everyone has to "unweave" themselves. By this time the frozen washcloth begins to get limp, which adds to the fun.

Some people play this game using actual frozen hot dogs or large frozen dill pickles!

133. Marshmallow Creations

Supplies: marshmallows, toothpicks
Optional: uncooked spaghetti

Even if you constantly tell your children, "Don't play with your food!" you might reconsider after doing this activity. Creating marshmallow sculptures is an easy way to keep children occupied while you try to make dinner or talk on the phone in relative quiet.

Set out a bag of mini-marshmallows and a box of toothpicks. Tell your children, "Create!" That's all the instruction they'll need to start poking the toothpicks into the marshmallows and making sticky sculptures. Some children make several small sculptures, while others will keep connecting pieces to make a giant tabletop masterpiece. Keep the supplies handy and let them add to the sculpture whenever they have a few extra minutes. Children enjoy this unstructured activity and also learn about weights and balance as they maneuver the marshmallows to connect with each other.

A simple variation on this activity is to use regular-size marshmallows. Bring out uncooked spaghetti to use as connectors between the marshmallows. Of course, cleanup is easy: just eat the marshmallows!

134. Crazy Utensil Meal

Supplies: assortment of kitchen utensils, empty box

Here's an activity guaranteed to be a great photo opportunity. There's something priceless about seeing Dad trying to eat meatloaf using a soup ladle. Just don't try this when stuffy Aunt Edna comes over or she'll question your sanity.

The next time you want to add a bit of fun to an ordinary meal, hide the silverware. Instead, collect kitchen utensils and put them in a box. Include anything that is safe, such as wooden spoons, slotted spoons, soup ladles, or salad tongs.

As the family sits down to dinner (and starts wondering why no silverware is on the table), bring out your Crazy Utensil Box. One at a time, each family member reaches inside, without looking, and selects an item. Whatever they pick...that's their eating utensil. Have you ever seen someone try to eat rice using a garlic press? Your family will be laughing so much they won't even notice that you're serving leftovers.

135. Decorate a Dry Bagel

Supplies: stale bagels, markers, stickers, glue, craft odds and ends

Children love the chewy taste of fresh bagels. Add some cream cheese and you have a snack the entire family enjoys. Yet, open that same bag of bagels a few days later and you find yourself with tire-shaped rocks. Instead of breaking a tooth trying to eat the bagel, turn it into a circular canvas for creativity.

Pass out the bagels, cautioning everyone not to throw them at each other. A stale bagel on the head could result in serious injury! Bring out an assortment of items ranging from buttons to toy cars to chenille stems to scraps of yarn. Children use glue to decorate their bagel in the most unique way possible. Create a bagel lion by gluing pieces of yarn around the bagel edge to form a mane. Cover a bagel with black paint to make a road for tiny cars. Add a fuzzy red pom-pom in the center of the bagel and make a clown face. Make squiggly pipe-cleaner worms that appear to be crawling out the center hole.

After the bagels are decorated, place them on your kitchen table for a truly one-of-a-kind centerpiece. Then go buy fresh, edible bagels to eat for breakfast.

136. Hearts for Everyone

Supplies: heart-shaped metal cookie cutters
Optional: pancake batter, sandwiches, cooked rice,
cheese slices, cookie dough, paint, heavy paper

Some days your heart seems to burst with love as you look at your child helping his little sister tie her shoes. You want to shout, "Jason, I love you so much!" Instead you contain yourself and pat him on the back as he walks by.

Instead of screaming your feelings of adoration, use a heart-shaped cookie cutter to demonstrate your love.

◆ When making pancakes in the morning, hold the cookie cutter firmly on the pan. Pour in the batter for tiny heart-shaped pancakes.

◆ As you make lunch sandwiches, get rid of those yucky crusts. Use the cookie cutter to cut heart-shaped sandwiches.

◆ Make rice for dinner. Place the cookie cutter on a plate and pack with rice. Carefully remove the cutter for perfect heart rice molds.

◆ Lay out slices of cheese. Form hearts by cutting with the cookie cutter.

◆ Here's a novel idea: use the cookie cutter to make heart-shaped cookies!

◆ Dip the cookie cutter in paint. Use as a stamp to decorate a heart-design card.

137. Popping Popcorn Mania

Supplies: popcorn (popped and unpopped), film canisters, Popsicle sticks, bowls, spices, cupcake or muffin tins, masking tape, markers, large needle and thread

Since popcorn is high on most people's snack list, find some new ways to enjoy this versatile food. You can have an entire afternoon of popping good fun.

The next time your family wants to munch on some popcorn, surprise them with some of these activities:

- Fill a plastic film canister with unpopped popcorn. See who can get closest to guessing the number of kernels inside.
- Play an indoor version of popcorn baseball. Set up three bases, fairly close together. The pitcher tosses a piece of popped popcorn as the batter tries to hit a home run using a Popsicle stick.
- Pass out bowls of plain, unsalted popcorn and a variety of spices. Everyone has ten minutes to come up with a new type of seasoning for their popcorn. Encourage children to come up with new names for their concoctions. Sample each other's culinary delights.
- Using masking tape, label each section of a cupcake or muffin tin with random point values. Take turns tossing single popped kernels into the muffin tin to accumulate the most points.
- Use a large needle and thread to string stale, leftover popcorn. Hang outside as a present for the birds.
- Don't forget to sit down with a bowl of popcorn and watch a family movie together.

crazy Cooking

138. Indoor Mini-S'mores

Supplies: any number of children, votive or pillar candles, matches, old newspapers, toothpicks, mini-marshmallows, chocolate chips, graham crackers

It's raining. You've played card games, watched videos, and the children are still antsy. Solution? Make some indoor s'mores. Don't worry, you don't have to build a blazing bonfire in the middle of the living room. With a little adult supervision, children can roast marshmallows safely on the kitchen table.

Gather several "chubby" candles so each child has their own. Cover the table with old newspapers in the event of a wax spill. Here's the gimmick: let the children poke toothpicks into miniature marshmallows and slowly roast them over the candle flame! While the marshmallows are turning golden brown, simply break graham crackers into small pieces. Children place their mini-marshmallow on the graham cracker, add a chocolate chip or two, and cover with the other graham cracker. Yum! A tiny, tasty s'more. (You can also melt chocolate chips in the microwave for ten to fifteen seconds and then spread the melted chocolate on the graham crackers.)

If you think back to camping trips, most children enjoy the process of *making* the s'mores better than actually eating them. Making indoor mini-s'mores, children take time slowly roasting their marshmallows over the candle flame. An added benefit is that children are usually very quiet while toasting the marshmallows. Ahhh, the sweet sound of silence!

139. Banana Bake

Supplies: source of heat, aluminum foil, unpeeled bananas, chocolate chips

The next time you have a barbecue, make good use of the heat after your steaks are cooked. A few basic ingredients let children make their own gooey dessert with only a bit of supervision.

Give each child a piece of aluminum foil about 10" x 12". With the peel on, slice a banana for each child lengthwise, taking care not to cut through the peel on the bottom. Gently spread the two sides apart so you have room to add your sweet ingredients. Place the banana on the foil. Sprinkle chocolate chips inside the slit. For a really sweet dessert, add miniature marshmallows also. Wrap the foil firmly around the banana and place it on the grill or stove top on warm heat. After about ten minutes, the banana bake is complete. An adult should unwrap the foil while children get the chance to eat their creation. The combination of warm banana and melted chocolate also makes a great topping over a bowl of vanilla ice cream.

140. Eat a Dirty Snack

Supplies: clay flowerpot, aluminum foil or plastic wrap, chocolate sandwich cookies, rolling pin, resealable bags, chocolate pudding, gummy worm

If you are a conscientious parent, your children eat only fresh fruit and vegetables for snacks. However, if you are like many of us, your children can be found consuming candy and chips on a regular basis. Instead of feeling guilty about serving children junk food, turn the process into a family activity by making dirt pudding. That way you have quality family time and a creative snack.

Provide a small clay flowerpot for each person. Wash off any bugs or dirt inside the pot. Some families purchase a set of new clay pots to keep on hand just for serving dirt pudding. When the pots are reasonably clean, line them with aluminum foil or plastic wrap.

Place several chocolate sandwich cookies in a resealable bag. Let your children crush the cookies with a rolling pin. Sprinkle a layer of cookie crumbs in the bottom of each pot. Crush enough cookies to make several layers and sprinkle on top. In the meantime, mix a batch of instant chocolate pudding. Pour a few spoons of pudding in each pot. Continue to layer cookie crumbs and pudding until the pots are full, then sprinkle a last layer of crushed cookies on top for a realistic dirt effect. Add a gummy worm and enjoy your dirty snack.

141. Year-Round Chubby "Snow" People.

Supplies: large and small marshmallows,
frosting (purchased or homemade), toothpicks,
mini M&Ms, scissors, fruit leather, Hershey's
Kisses, pretzel sticks

Who says you can only make snowmen (or snowpeople) in winter? Try creating this marshmallow snack anytime for year-round "frosty" fun.

Set out a variety of items to create a whole family of snow people. Stack three same-sized marshmallows on top of each other, using frosting to "glue" them together. The large marshmallows create adult snow people, while three miniature marshmallows represent snow children. Dip a toothpick into frosting and use it to attach the appropriate colored mini M&Ms for eyes, nose, and mouth. Use scissors to cut the fruit leather into long narrow strips to wrap around the snow person's "neck" as a scarf. For a warm hat, place a Hershey's Kiss on the large marshmallow and a chocolate chip on top of the mini-marshmallow head. Poke pretzel sticks in the sides for arms. Display your snow family until they disappear into someone's mouth.

142. Funny Family Fortunes

Supplies: paper, pencil, 1 egg white, 1/4 cup sugar,
1 tablespoon water, 2 tablespoons melted butter,
1/4 teaspoon vanilla, 1/3 cup flour, measuring
cups and spoons, mixing bowl, cookie sheets,
oven, muffin tin

When you go out for Chinese food, everyone enjoys reading the fortunes from the fortune cookies. Children love getting that tiny slip of paper saying, "Something very, very good will soon happen to you." Create your own fortune-cookie factory in the comfort of your own kitchen.

Before baking the fortune cookies, have the family make up silly or lighthearted fortunes and write them on thin strips of paper. A few examples:

- The next time you sneeze, a pimple will appear on your nose.
- The odor from your feet will soon disappear.
- Your beautiful smile will attract many bugs.
- Sing a song and the bluebird of happiness will land on your head.

Follow this easy recipe and insert your funny family fortunes:

1. Preheat the oven to 350° F.
2. Mix egg white with sugar in a small bowl.
3. Mix in water, melted butter, and vanilla.
4. Stir in flour.
5. Drop spoonfuls of the dough onto greased cookie sheets.
6. Spread the dough into very thin circles.
7. Have an adult put the cookies in the oven and bake three to five minutes or until lightly browned.

Remove cookies from oven and place a paper fortune in the center of the warm cookies. Fold the sides in over the fortune, bend each cookie seam side out, and place inside a muffin tin to hold the shape. Work quickly, because once cookies harden, it's difficult to get the traditional "folded cookie" shape. Remove the cookies and place a folded fortune in the middle of each. Let cool and enjoy your wacky fortunes.

143. Crispy, Crunchy Snacks

Supplies: cookie sheet, cookie cutter, flour
tortillas, salt, cinnamon, sugar

Some parents spend hours in the kitchen teaching children the fine art of gourmet cooking. It's never too much work to create appetizers of layered puff pastry covered in home-made shrimp sauce. Then, of course, there are those parents looking for quick and easy snacks without a culinary extravaganza. With only minimum adult supervision, children can make these crunchy snacks in a variety of fun shapes.

Get out all of your cookie cutters. Preheat the oven to 350°F. Place a flour tortilla on a kitchen counter or cutting board. Pretend that the tortilla is cookie dough and cut out decorative shapes with the cookie cutters. Spray the tortilla cut-outs on both sides with butter-flavored cooking spray. Lay the cut-outs on a cookie sheet and sprinkle with salt or, if you want a sweeter snack, cinnamon and sugar. Bake for six to seven minutes, or until lightly browned. Have an adult remove the cookie sheet from the oven. Transfer the tortillas to metal racks to cool.

Enjoy your sweet or salty crunchy snack.

144. Chocolate Gooey Cone

Supplies: ice cream cones, caramels,
chocolate chips, marshmallow

You could have a gallon of ice cream in your freezer, and your children would still want to stop for an ice cream cone on the way home from soccer practice. Somehow a cone makes ordinary ice cream seem like a treat. This sugar-laden snack uses a cone to create a chewy treat.

Give each child one cone, either sugar or cake. (For a special treat, fill the cones with pieces of fresh broccoli and carrots. Your children will love it...okay, maybe not.) Bring out the chocolate chips and caramels. Unwrap three or four caramels and put them in the cone. Top with a quarter cup of chocolate chips. As long as you're adding all this sugar, top everything with one large marshmallow. Keep the cone upright by placing it in a glass. Have an adult put the glass in the microwave for about fifteen seconds.

Your chocolate gooey cone will have layers of great taste!

145. Sweet Spoons

Supplies: spoons, chocolate chips, microwave, bowl, waxed paper, plate or cookie sheet

Fancy gourmet stores sell packages of stirring spoons covered with chocolate. You stir your warm drink and let the softened chocolate melt into the drink or on your tongue. Instead of paying gourmet prices, make your own.

If you want to make a large number of sweet spoons, use plastic spoons and double the recipe. Otherwise, just lay out six to eight of your everyday spoons. Put spoons in the freezer for ten to fifteen minutes. Meanwhile, have an adult melt about one cup of chocolate chips in a bowl in the microwave for thirty to forty-five seconds. The chips retain their shape, so stir them to be sure they're melted.

Gently dip the "bowl" of your spoon into the melted chocolate. Make sure there's chocolate on both sides. (It's tempting at this point to start licking the spoon right away!) Place the spoons on a plate or cookie sheet covered with waxed paper and refrigerate. After the chocolate has hardened, store it in plastic bags for the next time you want extra chocolate in warm milk or hot chocolate. You can also melt peanut butter chips or butterscotch chips for another type of sweet spoon.

146. Simple Stained Glass Cookies

Supplies: sugar cookie dough, cookie cutters, cookie sheets, oven, rolling pin, spatula, medium mixing bowl, 3 small bowls or cups, 2 egg yolks, fork, food coloring, new small paintbrushes or toothpicks

They seem to mock you at every grocery store checkout counter—magazine covers emblazoned with perfectly shaped, intricately decorated cookies. The caption reads, "Cookie Decorating Tips for Children." (Has the editor ever tried to make cookies with a preschooler? Most four-year-olds just want to eat as much frosting as possible.) Here's a simple cookie-decorating recipe that cuts down on sugar and gives children the chance to display artistic capabilities.

Make a batch of sugar-cookie dough from a mix or your favorite recipe, or use slice-and-bake refrigerated dough. Roll out the dough on a lightly floured surface until it is a quarter-inch thick. Cut out dough using your favorite cookie cutters and place it on cookie sheets.

Let children help you mix the stained glass "paint." In a medium bowl, whisk two egg yolks with a fork until smooth. Divide the blended egg yolk among three small bowls or cups—you are making three colors of egg yolk paint. Add two to three drops of food coloring into each cup and stir well. Use new small paintbrushes or toothpicks to "paint" each cookie. If you like, use the hard end of the paintbrush to form indentations in the dough to separate colors.

Bake according to the cookie recipe. Cookies will look like intricately designed stained glass windows...or a modernistic hodge-podge of colors.

147. Crock-Pot Caramel Apples

Supplies: Crock-Pot, apples (about 12 to 14), two 14-oz. packages of caramels, water, wooden spoon, Popsicle sticks, greased waxed paper, small bowls, toppings such as chopped nuts, sprinkles, mini chocolate chips, and coconut
Optional: markers

Check the very back of your kitchen cupboard. You'll probably find a Crock-Pot hidden behind the fondue pot and the pressure cooker. While traditional recipes call for using a double boiler, the Crock-Pot is a safer way to melt caramels around children.

After dusting off the Crock-Pot, keep your children occupied unwrapping two fourteen-ounce packages of caramels. Add the caramels to the Crock-Pot along with a quarter cup of water. Let the caramels melt for one to one and a half hours on high heat, stirring occasionally. In the meantime, set up your caramel-apple assembly line.

Set out small bowls filled with toppings such as chopped nuts, sprinkles, mini-chocolate chips, coconut, etc. Wash and dry the apples. If you need to pass time until the caramels melt, let the children use markers to decorate their Popsicle sticks with distinctive patterns and designs.

When the caramel is smooth and melted, help your children poke a Popsicle stick into the center of an apple and dip it into the melted caramel. Scrape off extra gooey caramel dripping from the apple before dipping into the toppings. Let cool on greased wax paper for ten to fifteen minutes. There's nothing like biting into a homemade caramel apple covered with chocolate chips and sprinkles.

Note: this recipe can be halved; since the caramel won't be as deep for dipping purposes, the caramel can be spread onto the apples instead.

Crazy Cooking

148. Magic Mosaic Bread

Supplies: bread dough, food coloring (preferably paste), flour, greased baking sheet, oven

Children love playing with clay or play dough. It's such a liberating feeling to roll, punch, poke, and squeeze the dough. Here's a way for children to mix and mold an edible version of play dough.

Provide your children with plain white bread dough and a lightly floured work surface. You can:

- ✿ Make dough from scratch, using your favorite bread recipe. (Time-consuming)
- ✿ Make dough in your automatic bread machine. (Easier)
- ✿ Purchase frozen bread dough at the store and let it defrost. (Easiest)

Divide the dough into four sections. Add a few drops of concentrated food coloring paste (available in stores carrying cake decorating supplies) to three sections of dough. Liquid food coloring also works, but the colors will be less intense. Help your children knead the dough to blend in the colors.

Here's where the children get to poke and prod. Give them chunks of colored dough, along with some of the plain dough. Let them make their own loaf of mosaic bread. Use the dough just like play dough, making abstract shapes, animals, or sea creatures.

After all the handling, let the bread rise in a warm place on a greased baking sheet for about an hour. Bake according to directions and enjoy eating warm multicolored bread.

149. Delightful Deviled Egg

Supplies: 12 hard-boiled eggs, medium mixing bowl, whipped cream cheese, fork, spoon, butterknife, olives, toothpick, ketchup

Deviled eggs are a traditional dish at potlucks and family get-togethers. Why not create a conversation piece the next time you take a dish to Uncle Ed's birthday party? Bring "Bloodshot Eyeballs" instead of ordinary deviled eggs.

Boil one dozen eggs. After the eggs have cooled, let your children help you peel them. Cut the eggs in half length-wise and gently scoop out the yolks. In a medium bowl, soften four ounces of whipped cream cheese and stir until smooth. Add one tablespoon of egg yolk to give the mixture a light yellow color, mixing well. Spoon cream cheese mixture into the hollowed-out egg white. Use a butter knife to smooth the surface. Press a green or black olive in the center for the "eyeball."

Have fun dipping a toothpick in ketchup and carefully drawing thin blood vessels in the cream cheese to resemble bloodshot eyes. These are guaranteed to be a long-remembered potluck dish!

Crazy Cooking

150. Tooty-Fruity Candle Salad

Supplies: plate, lettuce, pineapple rings, banana, maraschino or regular cherries, toothpick, knife

As conscientious parents, we try to provide healthy snacks for our children. But set out a bowl of fresh fruit, and what happens? The fruit attracts fruit flies before attracting any children. Here's a child-friendly fruit salad your children can create, display, and then eat.

Give your child a small plate as the base for his candle. Cover the plate with a few pieces of lettuce. Stack two or three rings of sliced pineapple to serve as the candleholder. Peel a banana and cut off an inch from each end so you have a straight banana piece. (Eat the curved ends.) Cut it in half lengthwise. Stand one banana piece in the center of the pineapple rings. Use a toothpick to attach the cherry "flame" to the top of the banana. Let your candle burn during dinner and then eat it with your fingers—sure beats eating a plain banana taken from the fruit bowl!

151. Chocolate-Covered Pretzels

Supplies: large pretzel sticks, 1 cup chocolate chips,
1 tablespoon butter, glass measuring cup, microwave,
egg carton, wooden spoon, small plates, toppings
such as sprinkles, chopped nuts, and coconut

Specialty candy shops often display thick, chocolate-covered pretzel sticks. Give this recipe a try. Children enjoy dipping the pretzels in chocolate and rolling them in special toppings.

Before you make your crunchy treat, make your own unique "Pretzel Drying Rack." Turn an empty egg carton upside down. Using the end of a wooden spoon, poke a hole in the center of each egg cup. This forms the holder where you'll put your chocolate-covered pretzels to set.

In a two-cup glass measuring cup, melt chocolate chips with butter in the microwave. Begin with twenty-five to thirty seconds. Stir and microwave in twenty-second increments until the chips are melted and smooth. While the chocolate cools slightly, set out several small plates filled with sprinkles, chopped nuts, coconut, or other toppings.

Children can dip one end of a pretzel stick in the chocolate, and then roll it in a topping. It's fun to make various combinations. Set each decorated pretzel stick into your drying container until the chocolate has cooled—then crunch away!

152. Artistic Pancakes

Supplies: pancake batter, plastic squeeze
bottle, frying pan, stove

Instead of spending extra money at a pancake restaurant, amaze your children with your designer pancakes. Tell them you went to the Courdon Bleu School of Pancakes!

Mix up your regular recipe for pancakes. Pour about a half-cup of batter into a plastic squeeze bottle. (You need a bottle that lets you "draw" with pancake batter. Often dollar stores sell squirt bottles for ketchup or mustard that work.) Heat the frying pan. Begin your designer pancakes by making a simple smiley face. Squirt the pancake batter in the pan so you have two eyes and a wide smile. Cook until golden brown. Gently pour batter on top of your pancake face as if making a normal pancake. Turn when bubbles appear in the dough. As you flip the pancake, you'll see how the face appears darker than the rest of the pancake.

Now that you have the technique, get busy with your pancake squirt bottle. Make fancy faces or free-form designs. To really impress your children, write their names with the squirt bottle. Just remember to make the letters backward. (On second thought, that's too much work!)

153. Crunchy Peanut Butter Sandwiches

Supplies: apple, knife, cutting board, peanut butter, mini-marshmallows, raisins

What child doesn't love peanut butter and jelly sandwiches? To give a twist to a traditional lunchtime favorite, substitute apple slices for bread.

An adult should core the apple. Peel the apple if your children like their apples "naked." Slice the apple crossways into an even number of rings (about four to six) and spread half the rings with a layer of peanut butter. Place five or six miniature marshmallows or raisins on the peanut butter. Gently press another slice of apple on top for a crunchy peanut butter and apple sandwich that's sure to be a hit.

As an extra treat, offer to impress your children with your ability to be a "starmaker." Cut an uncored apple in half crossways (not from stem to bottom). As you pull the two pieces apart, the apple seeds form a perfect star shape on each half. Give them to your children with the inspirational message that they should "reach for the stars" to achieve what they want in life. Hey, it works for Oprah!

154. Freeze It and They Will Eat It

Supplies: freezer, assorted small plastic containers, ice cube trays, fruit, juice, yogurt, plastic spoons, toothpicks

You're having a relaxing afternoon, reading in the backyard with your children on a hot summer day. Suddenly that familiar tinkling sound of the ice cream truck disturbs the peace. "Can I get a fudgsicle? I just have to get the twistee Popsicle!" Instead of doling out money for overpriced ice cream treats, let children create their own.

Set out a variety of small plastic containers. Use toothpicks as the holders for ice cube tray Popsicles. Add a plastic spoon to serve as the "stick" in empty yogurt containers. If you want centered handles, let the juices partially freeze before inserting the toothpick or spoon.

Children make their own frozen concoctions using whatever they think will taste delicious. Add a semi-educational twist and ask each child to label their specialty dessert. If Lauren puts orange juice and strawberry slices into a yogurt container, have her label it with something like, "Orange and Red Frozen Delight."

Pour juices, lemonade, chocolate milk, or even pudding into the containers. Add a few berries or stir in flavored yogurt. Let freeze for several hours and you have a neverending supply of frozen goodies. Over the summer, keep track of which combinations are the most popular.

155. Rock and Roll Ice Cream

Supplies: resealable plastic bags, high-sided bowl, measuring cups and spoons, 1/2 cup milk, 1/2 cup half-and-half, 1 tablespoon sugar, 1/4 teaspoon vanilla, 2–3 tablespoons rock salt, 2 cups ice cubes

Here's how to get rid of your children's excess energy. Instead of scooping up some ice cream from the freezer, have children make their own. You don't even need an ice cream maker because your children's movements churn the ingredients.

Put one sandwich-sized resealable bag inside another for extra strength. Place the double bags in a high-sided bowl for stability when children pour in the ingredients. Add milk, half and half, sugar, and vanilla. Squeeze out all the air and firmly seal both bags. Put the smaller bags inside a gallon size resealable bag. Cover with rock salt and ice. Seal this larger bag as well.

Let children take turns shaking, jiggling and even throwing the bag (carefully!). Put on some lively music and have children rock and roll while holding the bag. The more they move, the faster the milk turns to ice cream. After ten to twelve minutes, the ice cream will be ready to eat. It won't get rock hard, but will be soft and creamy enough for everyone to enjoy.

156. Chocolate Balloon Nests

Supplies: small balloons, large bowl, waxed paper, cookie sheet, chocolate chips, stove, double boiler, scissors

Looking for a unique way to serve dessert? How about making edible chocolate bowls? They're so good you might just serve the bowls without anything inside.

Begin the process by blowing up several balloons and tying the ends. Unless you want extra large bowls, use five-to seven-inch balloons. Place waxed paper over a cookie sheet. Have an adult use a double boiler to melt two 12-oz. bags of chocolate chips. If you want white bowls, simply use white chips. When the chocolate melts, remove from heat and pour into a bowl. You want to cool the chocolate slightly without getting it so cool it hardens into a solid mass.

Hold balloon at the tied end and dip in the chocolate, covering the entire bottom and halfway up the balloon. Gently put the chocolate covered balloons on the prepared cookie sheet. Place in refrigerator and chill until chocolate hardens.

After chocolate is solid, have an adult use sharp scissors to pop the balloon and remove it. You now have an edible bowl. Fill with ice cream or pudding, or simply munch away at the bowl!

157. World's Largest Banana Split

Supplies: rain gutter, plastic bowls and spoons, bananas, ice cream, toppings

This event has been done with groups consisting of several thousand people, but hopefully your group is smaller. Otherwise, you'll need a truckload of bananas. Children delight in sitting on the ground, eating a banana split out of their giant dish.

For obvious clean-up reasons, you'll want to be outdoors for this event. After you know the approximate size of your group, calculate how much rain gutter you'll need. Yes, rain gutter. Allow about one foot of rain gutter per person. You're probably thinking, "I don't happen to have seventy-five feet of extra rain gutter in my storage closet." No problem. Go to your local friendly hardware store and explain that you are having the world's largest banana split party. More than likely, they are happy to let you "buy" the rain gutter and return it the next day. Many times the store manager simply takes your name and address and asks you to bring the gutters back soon. After all, anyone that is crazy enough to put ice cream in a rain gutter can't be a devious thief.

Congratulations! You have your rain gutters! Lay them out, overlapping the ends. If you don't have room for a continuous straight line, just make a zigzag effect. For sanitary reasons, purchase lightweight paper or plastic bowls and squish them inside the rain gutter. Some ice cream parlors have narrow plastic boat-shaped bowls they'll sell you which fit nicely into the gutter.

Make sure everyone has arrived before bringing out the ice cream. Occupy the children with an organized event while you and several volunteers assemble the banana split. Slice bananas lengthwise and have one helper put pieces in each bowl. Work quickly and scoop ice cream into each bowl. Another helper follows with chocolate sauce, someone else dribbles on strawberries, and some lucky volunteer sprays whipped cream on top. Stick plastic spoons on top.

Call in the troops and watch the fun as everyone gets on the ground and digs into their ice cream. This is a great photo opportunity. Cleanup is simple: dispose of the bowls and hose down the rain gutters. (Store managers aren't too happy when you bring back the gutters covered with chocolate sauce.)

158. Eating Stone Soup

Supplies: pot, stove, vegetables, bouillon or broth, three smooth stones, bowls, spoons

Stone Soup is a favorite story with children. They can see the craftiness in the beggar's attempt to get a decent meal. (Not that we advocate tricking people into believing something that isn't true!)

Invite a group of children to a stone soup feast. Ask them to bring a vegetable to add to the delicious soup. When children arrive, take turns washing and chopping vegetables. Ahead of time, prepare a simple bouillon or broth to serve as the base for your soup.

Read *Stone Soup* to the children. Make a dramatic production out of the three smooth stones *you* have. Show children the stones and let them pass the stones around so everyone gets a chance to touch them. Proceed to act out the story. Show your pot of broth. After washing the three stones, add them to the soup. Let children take turns adding vegetables, just like in the story. While vegetables are cooking, play a few games or let children decorate plastic disposable soup bowls.

Serve the soup along with crackers or bread. When children comment how tasty the soup is, tell them that the secret ingredients are the three smooth stones.

159. Sensational Snow Creatures

Supplies: snow
Optional: costumes, plastic bowls, funnels and cups,
aluminum foil, squirt bottles, food coloring

It's snowing! Finally your children can look for long-lost mittens and hats and go play in the snow. Naturally, they'll start making a snowman. But wait. How about making a snow child? A snow dog? Why not a snow serpent?

While children enthusiastically roll snowballs, ask them for suggestions about other snow characters. It won't take long for them to come up with ideas. Here are some more suggestions:

- ☺ A traditional snowman is transformed into a Snow Princess with the use of an aluminum-foil crown and a ball gown from the costume box.
- ☺ Roll ten to twelve snowballs side by side. Add sticks for antennas to make a snow caterpillar. You could get authentic and add a hundred small sticks to represent tiny centipede legs.
- ☺ Bring out plastic storage containers, funnels, and paper cups to create special shapes. Pack snow into the container and invert. If the snow is damp enough, the shape slides right out.
- ☺ Make a traditional three-ball snowman. Fill several squirt bottles with water and a few drops of food coloring. Set the spray to "mist" and spray the snowman, dyeing the snow. Neighbors will wonder how you made a tie-dye snowman! Or use the steady stream on a spray bottle to write names in the snow. Make a batch of snowballs and spray each one a different color. Go really wild and spray the yard so it looks like a patchwork quilt!

160. Snowball Skill Throw

Supplies: snow, hula hoop, boxes, cans, cardboard, scissors

Ahhh, winter. Tiny flakes of snow drift silently to the ground. Everything is so peaceful...until a group of children begins a snowball fight. Then the noise and excitement reaches a feverish pitch, usually with someone crying after he gets hit in the face with a snowball.

Instead, avoid injuries and encourage children to channel their snowball-throwing skills with these activities, using ordinary household items.

- ◆ Hang a hula hoop from a tree or swingset and have children throw snowballs through the hoop. Draw several lines in the snow. Younger children stand closer to the target, while older ones need to throw from a farther distance.
- ◆ Place a box upside down in the snow. Stack several empty cans on top of each other in a pyramid. Children try to knock the cans over with snowballs.
- ◆ Cut apart a large cardboard box so you have a flat piece of cardboard. Cut five or six holes of various sizes in the cardboard. Use a permanent marker to designate a point value for each hole. Small holes get five points, larger holes get two or three points. Hang the cardboard where children can throw snowballs through the holes and add up scores. The cardboard should last for at least an afternoon's worth of snowy fun before disintegrating.
- ◆ If you have a solid garage door or a side of the house without any windows, make a giant target. Use chalk and draw circles like a dartboard, complete with a bull's-eye. Children try to hit the center of the target with snowballs.

161. Snowman Restaurant

Supplies: snow, assorted fruits, cereal, birdseed

The next time snow begins to fall, get ready to open a new restaurant. Don't worry, you don't need to get a business license yet. This restaurant is strictly for the birds.

As snow drifts down, help children look for misplaced boots and mittens so they can go outside and build a snowman. As soon as the snowman (or snowwoman) is ready, it's time for the grand opening of your restaurant. Decorate the snow person with fruit and seeds to serve as a feeding spot for your feathered friends. Some suggestions:

- Cut an apple into slices. Use a large needle and yarn to string the apple as a necklace for the snow woman.
- Outline the eyes with raisins.
- Spread peanut butter on stale bread. Place the slices in front of the snow person to form shoes.
- Use a plastic plate as a hat on the snowman's head. Fill the plate with birdseed or cereal.
- Clusters of dried cranberries make delectable buttons on the snowman's chest.
- Make an indentation in the face. Place a peeled banana in the space as a smile.
- Don't forget the carrot for a nose.

Watch as the birds arrive at your restaurant. You may end up with so many satisfied customers that you have a naked snowman!

Winter Fun

162. Crazy Snow Characters

Supplies: snow, sticks, rocks, costumes,
two or more people

The minute it begins to snow, children yell, "Let's make a snowman!" Three balls of snow, a carrot nose, and you have a snowman that looks like all the others in the neighborhood. This winter, create some snow characters with personality.

Set your children loose in the snow. Designate an area for each child in which to build their snow character, slightly away from all the others. Ask each child what friend or famous person they would like to create out of snow. Someone might want to make a tall snowman that looks like Michael Jordan. Another child might make a "snow-baby" of his infant sister. Encourage the children to embellish their character with twigs, rocks, or pieces of clothing.

After an allocated amount of time, walk around as a group, trying to guess the true identities of your snow characters.

163. Sneaky Snow Course

Supplies: snow, balls, assorted plastic cups and bowls, boards, hula hoops, hockey sticks or brooms

The next time it snows, transform your yard into a combination golf and obstacle course. Children will spend hours building the course and then playing in it.

Set out an assortment of plastic cups, bowls, boards, and balls. Encourage children to design a route for the balls to go through. They can use hockey sticks or brooms to maneuver their ball through the course. The course could start with a snow ramp with a cup stuck in the snow at the top for the first "hole." Lay a hula hoop on the snow and try to hit a giant hole-in-one.

If the snow packs firmly, make snow bridges for the ball to go under. Mini-snowmen can serve as obstacles. Keep bringing out garbage cans and other items. Children will incorporate them into their snow course.

164. Cozy Indoor Picnic

Supplies: tablecloth, picnic basket filled
with typical picnic food
Optional: Beach Boys music, swimsuits,
yellow paper sun

Nothing beats the old-fashioned fun of enjoying a picnic in the park on a summer day. Food tastes better and even the ants add to the atmosphere. The next time you are in the middle of a dreary winter day, re-create that summertime feeling in your living room.

Dig out your gingham tablecloth to set the stage for your indoor picnic. Can't find it? Give the children white paper and ask them to design placemats with a red and white gingham theme. Crank up the stereo with some Beach Boys music and, if you are really brave, invite everyone to eat in his or her swimsuits. (Adults usually compromise by wearing shorts.) Add to the picnic mood by cutting out a large yellow paper sun and hanging it from the ceiling.

The meal is typical picnic fare, served in a picnic basket, of course. The children can make sandwiches, mix lemonade, and set out bags of chips. The wind might be howling outside, but your family will enjoy a summer picnic on the floor of your cozy living room. After everyone is full, watch the smiles appear when you announce that dessert is s'mores made in the fireplace!

165. Pioneer Snow Ice Cream

Supplies: 4 cups snow, plastic bowls, mixing bowl and spoon, measuring cup and measuring spoons, 2 1/2 tablespoons milk, 1/3 cup sugar, 1/2 teaspoon vanilla extract

If you live in Palm Springs, this activity might be a bit difficult to do. However, if you live anywhere that gets even a few inches of snow, this recipe is sure to be an old-fashioned hit.

As the snow falls and children listen to the radio to see if school is cancelled, get ready to make super snow ice cream. Give children plastic bowls and turn them loose to collect four cups of clean snow. This may take several hours as children stop to build snowmen, throw snowballs, lose their gloves, etc. (They'll probably bring in more than four cups of snow just in their boots.)

Put the clean snow in a large bowl. Stir in milk, sugar, and vanilla extract. Explain to your children that the ice cream won't have the creamy flavor they are used to. Still, the early pioneers thought it was quite a tasty treat.

Taste a sample and add more sugar or vanilla to suit your family's taste buds. Scoop into bowls and eat your ice cream in front of the fire while reading *Little House on the Prairie*.

Winter Fun

Mad Scientists

166. Repeating Volcano

Supplies: mound of dirt or sand, empty tuna can or other small can, 3 tablespoons baking soda, 1/2 cup vinegar

No science fair would be complete without the famous exploding volcano, oozing flows of "lava" down the side. In most cases, an adult adds a combination of baking soda and vinegar, the papier-mâché volcano spews out foam, and then the adult cleans up the mess on the floor. By making an outdoor "family fun" volcano, your children can cause their own eruption, over and over again. The best part is that clean-up is minimal.

Begin by finding or making a mound of dirt outside. Don't worry about dirty fingernails. Let your children dig and make the volcano as big as they want. After the mountain is complete, have the children scoop out a small hole in the top, so that an empty tuna can fits inside. Pack the dirt around the sides of the can so it is as hidden as possible.

Here comes the fun part. Let your children spoon three or four tablespoons of baking soda into the can. Add a half-cup of vinegar and watch the lava flow down the mountain. After all the "oohhs" and "ahhhs" subside, show your children how to empty the tuna can and start all over again with another eruption. Sure, they'll use the entire box of baking soda and bottle of vinegar, but that's a small price for an afternoon of fun. Clean-up is simple: throw the tuna can in the recycling bin and spread the dirt back to ground level. This also works great at the beach.

Mad Scientists

167. Buzzing Balloon Rocket

Supplies: two trees or other well-anchored objects; string; long, hot-dog shaped balloons; tape; drinking straws

Children love to blow up balloons and then watch them buzz around the room while the air releases. The noise this makes is also very popular!

Tie one end of a sturdy string to a tree or other well-anchored object. Make sure another tree or anchor is available six to eight feet away to attach the other end. Thread a plastic drinking straw onto the string and tie the loose end of string to the other tree, making sure the string is tight. Slide the straw close to one tree.

Give your child a long, hot-dog shaped balloon and ask her to blow it up. Have an adult hold the end shut so that no air escapes. (It can be frustrating for children if they accidentally release the air ahead of time.) With the adult holding the inflated balloon, your child can tape the balloon (parallel to the ground, with balloon neck toward the nearer tree) onto the straw with two or three pieces of tape. Ask for a countdown. 10-9-8-7-6-5-4-3-2-1, blast off! Release the balloon and watch the air propel it smoothly along the length of string. Measure the distance and have family members try to beat the record.

Try this with a longer distance between trees and a larger balloon. This rocket really soars!

168. Big Bubble Blast

Supplies: shallow, wide dish; 6 cups water;
2 cups liquid dishwashing detergent; 3/4 cup
light corn syrup; 2 tablespoons glycerin
(optional, but helps produce stronger bubbles);
bubble makers, such as metal coat hangers

Blowing bubbles is a popular pastime for all ages. Many churches now request that wedding guests blow bubbles instead of throwing rice or birdseed! Rather than buying bubble solution, let children stir up a batch of their own.

For strong, long-lasting bubbles, combine the water, dishwashing detergent, corn syrup, and glycerin. Mix well and let sit overnight.

Pour some of the solution into a shallow container. Send the children on a tour of the house, looking for items to use as "bubble makers." Metal coat hangers bent into a circle, dipped in the solution, and waved overhead produce large bubbles. Use a rubber fly swatter and watch hundreds of tiny bubbles appear. One mother tripled the bubble solution and poured it in a plastic wading pool. Her children used a hula hoop for gigantic bubbles!

Mad Scientists

169. Rocket to Mars (or to the Neighbor's Backyard)

Supplies: unobstructed play area, plastic soda bottle, cork, crepe-paper streamers, thumbtacks or strong tape, measuring cup and spoons, 3/4 cup vinegar, 1/2 cup water, 1 tablespoon baking soda, funnel

It's difficult to understand the size and force of the space shuttle taking off at the Kennedy Space Center. Everything looks so small from the TV's perspective. Show your children how to make their own rocket. It might not fly to Mars, but it will take off with a big swoosh.

Go outside where you have plenty of space and no people casually walking by. Make sure you have a cork that fits snugly into a clean, plastic, liter soda bottle. Use thumbtacks or strong tape to attach crepe-paper streamers to the cork for decoration. You'll want to be able to see it shoot through the air. Make sure the bottle stands securely on a flat surface and children are at a safe distance.

Pour vinegar and water in the bottle. Place a small funnel in the bottle opening. Have an adult quickly add baking soda through the funnel. Move quickly! As soon as the baking soda goes down the funnel to the vinegar, toss the funnel. Plug the bottle firmly with the cork. Run! Keep children away as the bottle fills with pressure and shoots the cork streamer in the air. They'll want to do this over and over.

170. Super Simple Gliders

Supplies: paper, scissors, drinking straw, tape

Watch a group of children playing outside. It won't be long until they begin throwing balls, Frisbees, or whatever's available. There's a sense of freedom in having the power to make things soar through the sky. Before rocks start flying, help children make these lightweight gliders.

Cut two strips of paper. One should be 1"x 6", the other 1"x 8". Make two loops by taping the ends of each paper strip together. Lay the straw inside the loops and tape one circle onto each end of the straw.

Go outside and give your glider a gentle "toss." It should fly through the air. Experiment with different sizes of paper loops. What happens if you toss your glider with the small loop directed forward? Is it different than tossing it with the larger loop forward? What happens if you attach three paper strips to the straw? Try making a glider with smaller paper strips attached to tiny snack-juice straws.

Mad Scientists

171. Pint-Sized Pendulum Power

Supplies: swing, large piece of cardboard, wide marker

Children are interested in the designs pendulums make with sand or markers. Intricate designs are created as the pendulum swings in a symmetrical motion. Instead of watching a pendulum, let your child be a pendulum.

Find a large piece of cardboard, the bigger the better. A large box cut apart works well. Place the cardboard under a swing. Weigh down the corners with rocks to keep the cardboard from shifting.

Have your child lie on her stomach on the swing. She is now part of the pendulum. Once she's comfortable, give her a wide marker. She holds the marker in one position as you swing her side to side in the swing. Just make sure the marker comes in contact with the cardboard. A design will take place as the human pendulum moves. Push her in another direction and watch the design change also.

When the cardboard is covered with patterns, add newsprint on top and continue making pendulum art as long as your child stays comfortable.

172. Sink or Float?

Supplies: bucket or large bowl, water,
assorted household items
Optional: lump of modeling clay

Sometimes ordinary activities create surprises. Children have all seen pictures of large cruise ships floating on the ocean. Why does the cruise ship float when a small rock thrown in the water immediately drops to the bottom of the lake?

Get a plastic bucket or bowl and fill it halfway with water. Then go through the house and collect a variety of items such as toy cars, crayons, paper plates, sponges, etc. One at a time, show your child an item and ask, "Do you think this item will sink or float?" After they guess, have them put the item in the water to see the results. At times, you'll be surprised to find an item floating when you were sure it would sink.

For variety, have your child collect the items and then ask you if they will sink or float. Or, if you have a piece of clay handy, try this activity: roll the clay into a ball and watch it drop to the bottom of the bucket. Now form the clay into a bowl shape. Ask your child if the bowl will float, even though it weighs the same as the ball of clay. Let your child put the bowl in the water. Items that float push aside their own weight. The extra displaced water helps support the bowl so it doesn't sink.

173. Mad Scientists

Supplies: plastic tablecloth, plastic containers, rubber gloves, jug of water, food coloring, eyedroppers, coffee filters

Is there a budding scientist in your home? Do you have a child that loves to mix and stir various concoctions? Set her up with a miniature science lab and see what develops.

For best results, put a plastic tablecloth on the table. Give your child a plastic jug of water, several plastic containers, and bottles of food coloring. Provide rubber gloves if you don't want stained fingers. To add to the effect, provide eyedroppers or a turkey baster—it adds to the scientific atmosphere.

Let your scientist experiment. She'll mix colors, add water, and figure out how to create pastel colors. White coffee filters absorb colors well, so your child can try dipping edges of the filters in colored water.

After hours of colored fun, cleanup is simple. Just toss the colored water and save the food coloring (if any is left) for another day's experiment.

174. Stretched to the Limit

Supplies: small plastic container, paper towel, rubber band, coins, water, two or more players

"Stretched to the limit" sounds like a description of how some parents feel at the end of the day. Instead of feeling frustrated, involve your children in this game of concentration and suspense.

Set out an unbreakable container such as an aluminum can or margarine tub. Dampen a paper towel and squeeze out the excess moisture. Lay the wet paper towel over the container. Carefully slip a rubber band over the top of the container to keep the paper towel in place. The paper towel should be stretched tightly.

One at a time, take turns putting one penny after another on top of the paper towel. See how much weight the paper withstands before it rips. For variation, give each player his or her own cup with the stretched paper towel. Count who has the most pennies on his or her wet towel before it tears in half. For variety, try stretching the paper towel with dried beans, marbles, or even Lego pieces.

Mad Scientists

175. Homemade Pendulum

Supplies: paper cups, salt, string or yarn, dark paper

Many children's museums have elaborate pendulums where children swing funnels full of sand to create designs. With only paper cups, salt, and yarn, you can make a pendulum at home.

Poke a very small hole in the bottom of a paper cup. If you have access to a cup with a pointed bottom, like those found at a water cooler, snip off the very tip of the cup. Punch two holes on the top of the cup and string a twelve-inch piece of yarn through both holes. Tie the ends of yarn together to form a handle.

Lay down a piece of black or dark blue paper on a table or the floor. Fill the cup with two to three teaspoons of salt, holding your finger over the hole in the bottom of the cup. Place the cup over the paper. Hold the cup by the yarn handle and release the salt. Gently swing the cup from side to side, watching the salt flow to create a pattern on the paper. Swing the cup in different directions to change the design. What happens if you add flour or sugar to the cup?

176. Mystery Lava Soap

Supplies: small bowl, laxative tablets (such as Ex-Lax), rubbing alcohol, soap

If you've ever looked at a *National Geographic* magazine, you've seen pictures of glowing red lava oozing down an erupting volcano. Here's a chance to have red foaming lava flow from your hands. It's not as hot as real lava, of course!

Crush two Ex-Lax or other laxative tablets in a small bowl or cup. (Make sure the children don't eat the tablets.) You'll have an interesting discussion explaining just what laxatives are used for, and how they work. Add one teaspoon of rubbing alcohol to the crushed tablets. Stir well.

Rub the mixture on your hands. The alcohol will dry quickly. Just don't rub your eyes with alcohol on your hands. Go to a sink and pretend that your hands are normal. Slightly wet your hands and wash with soap. Watch out! You'll have foaming lava coming from your hands!

177. Dangerous New Dinosaurs

Supplies: chicken bones, water, pot, stove, cardboard, glue, markers

Children are fascinated with monstrous dinosaurs. They're big and make ferocious sounds. Since your local zoo probably doesn't have any live dinosaur exhibits, let your child make his own version of a prehistoric dinosaur.

In order to make this activity a success, you need a chicken. Purchase a large fryer and make your favorite recipe, or get a whole rotisserie chicken from the deli. After enjoying a good meal, put the chicken pieces with bones into a pot of boiling water. Cook for an hour until any remaining meat falls from the bones. Let cool and have your children pick out as many bones as possible. At first they might be squeamish, but will soon get the hang of collecting the bones. Wash the bones in soapy water and place them on a cookie sheet. Bake at 200°F for thirty to forty minutes.

As the bones are cooling, give the children pieces of cardboard or construction paper. Ask them to pretend they just captured a new type of dinosaur. What does it look like? Can it fly? Does it have horns? Sketch an outline of your dinosaur. Take the dried bones and glue them onto the sketch. Smaller bones cut easily to fit into tiny spaces. Use a brown marker to draw details on your dinosaur if you don't have enough bones.

Set up a miniature museum and display the prehistoric dinosaur bones!

178. Testing Your Senses

Supplies: bandana for blindfold, variety
of household objects, box or bag

Did you know that a box of new crayons is one of the top three most readily identifiable smells? See how well your children use their senses to identify a variety of objects.

Go through the house and collect an assortment of items ranging from an apple to a zebra (stuffed, of course!). Put the items in a box or bag so they remain hidden. Here are some ways to test your children's senses:

- Blindfold them and let them feel the objects. Can they tell the difference between a tomato and a nectarine?
- Place items in a paper bag. Try to guess the item by feeling it from the outside of the bag.
- While blindfolded, give your children objects to smell without touching them. Do potatoes have a smell? Can they identify the owner of a stinky shoe?
- Put a small item in an enclosed box. Shake the box back and forth. Can your children guess the item by the sound only?
- Blindfold your children and remove their shoes and socks. Place an item on the floor and see if they can guess the item by feeling it with their feet.

To end the game, divide the objects evenly among your children and see who can be first to put all the items back where they belong.

Mad Scientists

179. Turn Abe Lincoln Green

Supplies: pennies, saucer, vinegar, paper towel

Did you ever wonder why the Statue of Liberty has a green glow to her body? The copper in the metal she's made of reacts to oxygen, causing her gown and face to take on a greenish tint. You can get the same results by showing children how to turn Abe Lincoln green.

Cover the bottom of a saucer with vinegar. Fold a paper towel in fourths and place it on top to absorb the vinegar. Place several pennies on the paper towel, with Lincoln's face looking up at you. Let them stand overnight. Remove the pennies and look at poor President Lincoln's complexion! Vinegar is an acid that combines with the copper in the pennies to make a green coating called copper acetate. (Watch how impressed your children will be when you share your scientific knowledge.) It takes oxygen in the air for the chemical reaction to take place, which is why Lincoln's face turns green but the other side of the penny stays copper-colored.

180. Checking out
What's Inside

Supplies: old toasters, telephones, or computers;
screwdrivers; pliers

Remember how your toddler loved to take things apart to see how they worked? It was so cute when your two-year-old pulled the petals off your silk flowers or investigated the inside of a vase by dumping out the water. As children get older, they still need to explore and touch. With adult supervision, encourage them to see the inner workings of various toys and office supplies.

The next time you see a "Garage Sale" sign, pull over and check out the bargains. Look specifically for something your children could take apart. How about seeing what's inside an Etch-A-Sketch? Is there a telephone selling for a dollar? Buy it so your budding engineer can take it apart. Think what your child could learn by discovering the inner workings of an ancient computer.

After you've brought your items home, provide children with an assortment of screwdrivers and pliers. Many children are happy just working with "real" tools. They'll open panels, close them up again, and try to disconnect wires. (If children are working with electrical machines, cut each plug so they don't accidentally plug it in.) This can be an ongoing process, with children working on the item whenever the mood hits. One preteen happily took apart a manual typewriter, fascinated with the process of how the metal plates produced letters on paper. Don't worry if the machine never gets put back together. Even master mechanics end up with leftover parts!

Mad Scientists

223

181. Amazing Science Tricks

Supplies: baby food jar, uncooked rice, plastic knife,
Wint-O-Green Lifesavers, hand mirrors, spoons

Think about your deprived children: they never had a chance to sit in school and watch a black-and-white 16 mm film showing Mr. Wizard's science experiments. Remember how the smallest bit of science "magic" kept us enthralled? You probably can't even find 16 mm projectors anymore. But you can find books and websites with a variety of easy-to-do science experiments.

Ask your children to bring home books on science from the school library. Look through the activities together and select some you'd like to try. Instead of trying things together, assign each family member a project to practice and present to everyone else. Here are a few ideas you might use when putting on your science show in tribute to Mr. Wizard:

- ✷ Fill a small-necked jar (like a baby food jar) with uncooked rice. Pack rice firmly. Take a plastic knife and poke it into the rice fifteen to twenty times. Keep packing the rice down. It needs to be tightly packed. Now jab the knife to the bottom of the jar and slowly lift up. The friction keeps the rice packed against the knife so you can lift the jar.
- ✷ Give everyone a Wint-O-Green Lifesaver. Make sure it is not the sugarless type. Take two or three people at a time into a dark closet and bring along a mirror. After adjusting to the darkness for a few minutes, bite into the Lifesaver while holding the mirror in front of your face. You'll see sparks fly from your teeth. The crushed sugar crystals in the candy produce sparks.
- ✷ Give everyone spoons and ask them to balance the bowl of the spoon on their nose. Once you find the balance point, the spoon will hang.

182. Giant Bath Balls

Supplies: newspaper or old shower curtain, 4 Alka-Seltzer tablets, 4 tablespoons cornstarch, 1/2 cup baking soda, 6 tablespoons coconut oil (found in health food stores), 1/4 teaspoon essential oils
Optional: liquid food coloring

Walk by a store selling specialty soaps and lotions and you'll see giant balls guaranteed to make bathtime a bubbling experience. Gather together a few supplies and make your own version of bubbling bath balls. This also makes a great activity at a birthday party for preteens.

Cover the work area with an old shower curtain or newspaper. (Let's face it; anytime kids are at a table, something messy is bound to happen.) Crush the Alka-Seltzer tablets into fine powder. Add cornstarch and baking soda and mix well. In the microwave, have an adult melt the coconut oil. As it cools, add essential oil, any scent. If you wish, add a few drops of food coloring. Stir this into the dried mixture.

Use your hands to form the mixture into balls about the size of tennis balls. Roll until smooth. Let set overnight in a dry place. The next day, have your child get in the bathtub and drop your giant bath ball into the water for a foaming experience.

Mad Scientists

183. Miniature Crystal Caves

Supplies: shallow bowl or casserole dish,
charcoal briquettes, mixing bowl, measuring
spoons, 6 tablespoons salt, 6 tablespoons liquid
bluing (available in the laundry section of the
supermarket), 6 tablespoons water, 1 teaspoon
ammonia, food coloring

Television shows and magazines often offer glimpses of underground caverns. The huge chambers glisten with stalagmites and crystals. You don't have to visit a cave to experience shimmering crystals.

Set out a shallow bowl or casserole dish. Put in four or five charcoal briquettes. In a separate bowl, mix salt, liquid bluing, and water. Have an adult add ammonia. Pour this mixture over the charcoal. Add a few drops of different colored food coloring in various places on the coals. Let stand overnight away from young children.

Within twenty-four hours, small crystals will form. They'll continue to expand for several days. If it is a small dish, the crystals actually start growing over the edge. Use a plastic spoon to occasionally drip the water mixture back over the rocks. You now have a tabletop version of Carlsbad Caverns.

184. Shadow Creatures

Supplies: sunshine, chalk, tape measure

Remember as a child how you tried to jump on your shadow? Other times you simply marveled at the length of your arms and legs, as your elongated shadow seemed to stretch forever.

Since the sun's position changes as the earth moves around it, shadows change also. When the sun is overhead at noon, your child's shadow should be the shortest. Help your children enjoy the different sizes of their shadows throughout the day.

For best results, try this on a sunny day! In the early morning, have your child stand on a sidewalk or driveway while you trace around her shadow. Let her be creative by holding one hand in the air or standing on one foot. Label the time of day. Get a tape measure and measure her shadow.

At noon, repeat the process in the same or a nearby location, and then again in late afternoon. They'll enjoy striking a different pose each time. Compare and contrast the sizes of their shadows throughout the day. Let them use colored chalk to decorate the shadows by drawing facial features and clothing.

Mad Scientists

Are We There Yet?

185. Junior Tour Guides

Supplies: none

On most family vacations, parents announce the daily schedule. "Tomorrow we arrive at Grandma's house where we'll have a picnic with all your relatives. Be nice to Cousin Jeffrey, even if he is a whiner. That afternoon we'll go to the fair. The next day we'll hike to the waterfall where I proposed to your mother." Is it any wonder children complain about trips?

Before your next trip, consider involving children in some of the following ways:

☺ Brainstorm all the necessary preparations. Include items such as packing a deck of cards, stopping the mail, and collecting swimsuits.

☺ After you have a master list, assign jobs. Even a ten-year-old can call the kennel and make arrangements to board the dog. Just have an adult close by! Preschoolers are capable of wiping off dusty suitcases.

☺ Make a large calendar with completion dates for each task. Anyone can look at the calendar and see how many days they have to complete their duties.

☺ Get everyone's input about negotiable situations. Should the family start driving early in the morning so kids can sleep in the car? How do you determine seating arrangements? How much spending money does each child get?

☺ Ask older children to investigate the area you're planning to visit. Look up websites or call state tourist information centers. Children can plot out the route and see what tourist attractions are on the way.

☺ Use the trip as a learning experience. Give older children a set amount of money for the day.

231

They allocate money for meals, snacks, and lodging. It's an eye-opener for a twelve-year-old to start out with $200 and discover she has little left over after a day.

☺ If traveling by plane, allow children to find the ticket counter. Stand in the background as they hand over tickets and luggage. Let them lead you to the correct boarding gate. One family let their ten-year-old file his own lost luggage claim. It may take longer, but your child gains valuable skills. Just be sure to allow plenty of extra time.

☺ Many hotel rooms have tourist directories with discount coupons. Put children in charge of clipping coupons and split the savings with them.

These activities teach children valuable planning skills while adding to the anticipation of the trip.

186. Keep It Clean

Supplies: hanging plastic pocket-type shoe organizer
(available at discount stores), permanent marker,
duct tape, yarn or string

You are prepared! You've packed snacks, water bottles, and enough games to serve a camp. This trip will keep children so occupied they won't have a chance to be bored. It won't be long, however, before the backseat of your car is covered with crayons, loose cards, and action figures. Organize your children's things by using an inexpensive, hanging plastic shoe organizer. The pocket-like compartments provide a perfect storage solution for travel toys.

Cut apart the organizer into sections of three or four pockets per child, and label each with a child's name. Reinforce the top of each section with duct tape, and punch two holes. Thread yarn or string through the holes. Tie the string around the front seats so the pockets rest on the back of the front seats. When children sit in the back, all their travel supplies are hanging right in front of them for easy access.

Children will be able to reach their own snack or toy when they want it. And possibly, just possibly, they'll return each item to the designated compartment.

187. Travel Itinerary

Supplies: paper, pencil
Optional: map, highlighter

Imagine if someone said to you, "Tomorrow we're going for a long ride in the car to Baruga Lewinga." You would have no idea where you were going or for how long. Sometimes we tell our children they're going on a trip, but they have no understanding what that entails. Solve some of the "are we there yet?" problems by providing children with a fact-filled itinerary.

Travel agents provide customers with details about dates, times, and costs. Write up and pass out a modified list that gives children tentative information about the trip. For example:

> Friday evening: Finish packing. Put the suitcases by front door.
> Saturday morning 5:00 A.M.: Mom and Dad will put you in the car wearing your pajamas.
> Sleep in the car until about 7:30 A.M. Stop at a pancake house for breakfast in Olympia.
> Drive until 11:00 A.M. Jennifer rides in the front seat.
> 11:00 A.M. rest stop at Tacoma. Open a surprise gift.
> Drive until 12:30 P.M. Sam rides in the front seat.
> 12:30 P.M. Emily chooses our lunch location in Seattle area. Everyone gets a dollar to spend on treats.

The itinerary helps children feel they have an understanding of where and how things are happening. Give each older child a map and highlighter marker to plot the route also.

188. Puzzling Maps

Supplies: map, cardboard, glue, clear contact paper, resealable bag, highlighter

We've all gotten frustrated trying to fold a map in a cramped space. It should go back together in neat folds, but that seldom happens. Add fun to children's map reading by making a laminated map puzzle.

Begin by selecting just the area of the map needed. If traveling to Grandma's house four hours away, you don't need a map of the entire United States. Use a copy machine to enlarge or reduce the map area to about 8 1/2"x 11". (Unless of course, you are planning a trip around the world; then a larger map is certainly appropriate.)

Glue the map to a piece of lightweight cardboard. After the glue dries, cover with clear contact paper. Alternatively, most printers can laminate the map inexpensively. Cut the map into random shaped puzzle pieces, and store in a resealable plastic bag. When children want to know, "How long until we get there?" have them assemble the puzzle and check their location. Use a highlighter marker to plot how far you've already come.

189. Map Calculations

Supplies: maps

Solve the age-old complaint of "I'm tired of sitting in my seat" by distracting children with some map-related activities. To avoid tension, give each child the same map, or make color copies of just the route you are taking.

Ask some of these questions:

- Where are we right now?
- If we went twenty miles north, where would we be?
- Find the closest lake.
- Is there an ocean close by? If so, how many miles is it from where we are now?
- Where is the closest mountain range?
- Check the legend. What is the symbol for tourist attraction? Where's the nearest tourist attraction to us?
- Could we reach our destination following back roads?
- What is the mileage difference between traveling to our destination by freeway or back roads?

After your children tire of questions, see who can correctly fold their map in the shortest time.

190. For Testy Passengers

Supplies: cookie sheets, flannel, felt shapes, magnets, tape recorder

Tired of listening to squabbles from the back seat? Thinking you'll never go on a long car trip again? Instead of getting irritated with restless children, try these activities:

- Cover one side of an old metal cookie sheet with flannel. You now have an instant flannel board which children can use with an assortment of felt shapes and figures. Many school-supply stores sell complete kits of precut flannel board figures. When the kids get bored with felt shapes, turn the cookie sheet over to the metal side and hand out magnets. You could even start a collection of inexpensive magnets from souvenir shops along the way.

- The "Color-Song" game lets all ages participate. Select one person to begin by singing a song that mentions a color. Then the next person sings another song. Keep going until you run out of songs with a color. You'll be amazed how many songs you'll end up singing. Try *Rudolf the Red-Nosed Reindeer*, *Blue Suede Shoes*, *The Yellow Rose of Texas*, etc.

- Check out books on tape from the local library to help pass the time. Add a twist by bringing along a portable tape recorder and a blank tape. Let your backseat passengers sing, tell jokes, and interview each other while being recorded. They'll love listening to their own tape over and over.

- Pick a car in front of you and read out the license plate. Does it say something like RSD 362? Ask children to come up with a slogan or saying where each word starts with the letters on the license plate. RSD could be: Read Something Daily or Roger Skis Dangerously.

191. Homemade Bingo

Supplies: cardboard, marker, old magazines, blunt
scissors, glue stick, construction paper
Optional: coins

Passing the time in a positive way is a major objective when traveling with children in a car. Instead of simply buying a game of travel bingo, keep children occupied making their own game.

Before the trip, draw out a traditional bingo card grid on a piece of cardboard or paper with twenty-five squares, five down and five across. Leave all the spaces blank. Make one card for each family member. Cut small shapes from construction paper to use as markers. You also can give out nickels or dimes to use as markers. That way the children get some vacation spending money when they play the game.

When on the road, give each child a lapboard or other flat surface to work on. Pass out the bingo cards along with old magazines, blunt scissors, and a glue stick. Ask them to cut out pictures of things they might see outside the car window while driving down the road and glue them in each square. Examples are: trucks, cows, churches, stores, school, American flag, stop sign, etc. This alone should pass an hour or so. If you have artistic children, encourage them to draw the items in the squares. After all the squares are filled in (and your car is littered with scraps of paper), it's time to begin the game.

Pass out whatever you are using as markers. Everyone places their homemade bingo card on the flat surface and starts looking intently out the window. The minute they spot one of the items depicted on their card, they cover that space with a marker. The first person to cover a row of objects is the winner. Vary the game by seeing who can block each of the four corners or make a "picture frame" by having all the outside edges blocked.

192. Postcard Pastimes

Supplies: postcards, pencils, stamps, photo album

We all have good intentions to keep a travel diary while going on a trip. Often we get so busy we neglect to find time to record the daily events. Here are two ways to use post-cards to help children remember the highlights of their trip.

☼ Give your child a small daily "postcard allowance" so they can have the freedom to buy postcards on their own. Children feel responsible knowing they don't have to ask for every purchase they want to make. As your children buy postcards, help them write one or two sentences on the back, explaining why the card has significance. For example, after buying a postcard of a scary roller coaster, your child could write, "It was fun riding Thunder Thrill roller coaster. I especially liked listening to Mom as she screamed when we were turned upside down." If your child doesn't want to write comments, have an adult jot down a line or two. Then stamp and address the card to your child at home. Upon return from your trip, children have a collection of mail waiting for them, complete with a "diary" of each day's events.

☼ If you don't want to mail the postcards home, simply put them in photo album designed to hold 4" x 6" photos. The postcards fit right inside and the protective pages save postcards from juice spills. Since most postcards have a tendency to get lost anyway, the photo album provides an all-in-one storage case.

193. Fill in the Details

Supplies: none

Travel time is a wonderful opportunity to relive past vacations or family events. Use this game to help recall details from deep down in your memory.

Select a person to bring up an event that happened recently. It doesn't have to be a major occurrence, and even everyday events work fine. Perhaps the dog threw up on the new couch, or Grandpa came over to show off his new mountain bike.

For example, your son suggests talking about his birthday party last month. Take turns giving one detail about the party. At first, it's easy to recall events such as:

◆ Jason turned ten.
◆ It was raining.
◆ He had nine friends come over (list names).
◆ Mom served soccer-themed cupcakes.

As you continue the game, it becomes harder and harder to remember details. Keep going until no one can add more information. Make the game harder by picking an event that occurred eight or nine months ago and repeat the process. You'll be amazed at all the memories that are triggered trying to recall the event.

194. Tall Tales Picture Contest

Supplies: old magazines, construction paper, glue, scissors

This game requires a small amount of advance preparation on the part of an adult. However, if it results in a time of peaceful harmony from the backseat, isn't the extra work worth it?

Before your trip, collect an assortment of pictures from magazines. Try to select pictures that involve people in a variety of settings such as picnicking, decorating a Christmas tree, etc. (If you really want to impress your children with your advance preparation, glue the pictures on colored construction paper.)

When children get restless, announce with a great flourish that they are invited to participate in the "Tall Tales Picture Contest." Prizes will be awarded to all participants.

Ask for a volunteer. Hand the first child one of your pictures. They have to show the picture to the rest of the group and then make up the most outrageous "Tall Tale" they can. Perhaps they are holding a picture of two people sawing down a tree. The story might describe how, when no one is looking, lumberjacks cut down trees and then eat the entire tree. Usually each story gets more outrageous than the last. As children start to lose interest, announce the winners of the Tall Tales contest. Categories could include: Best Scary Story, Best Story that Made Us Laugh, Best Story Using Unusual Names, etc. Make sure everyone gets a prize, which can be as simple as getting to ride in the front seat or deciding where to eat dinner.

195. Lumpy Memory Book

Supplies: lightweight cardboard, stickers, markers, resealable sandwich bags, hole-puncher, yarn

"Mom! I want to take this pinecone home!"

"Don't throw away that ticket stub. I want to keep it!"

Being on a trip inspires children to become pack rats. Suddenly every brochure or souvenir wrapper takes on new significance. (Yet somehow all the items end up under the bed once you get home.) Let children make their own lumpy memory book.

These books can be constructed at home, or bring the supplies and have children make them while traveling. They may be occupied for twenty or thirty minutes!

- Give each child two pieces of lightweight cardboard about 4" x 6". Decorate these book covers with stickers or markers.
- Place together six to eight resealable plastic sandwich bags, with the sealed ends together.
- Place the bags between the book covers.
- With an adult's help, punch two holes through the cardboard and bottom of the bags.
- String yarn through the holes and tie securely. Careful! The sandwich bags get slippery.

Children can use the book to store priceless vacation treasures such as postcards, special small stones, and other memorabilia. Just open one of the bags, insert the item, and seal the bag again. Everything is easy to see and store.

196. Super-Saver Stones

Supplies: stones, permanent markers

Most families collect an assortment of items from vacations or even walks around the block. There's something reassuring about going someplace new and bringing home a memento from the experience. Instead of buying family members an embroidered sweatshirt from every excursion, start collecting something entirely free. How about starting a family rock collection?

Before you laugh, give it a try. Rocks come in all shapes, sizes, and textures. Many have distinct markings. Best of all, rocks are free. Next time you take a trip, explain to your family that you'll be coming home with a rock...a very special rock, of course. This will also be a lesson in democracy.

As you go on a local hike or visit the Grand Canyon, keep a sharp eye out for a distinctive rock. More than likely, several family members will claim to have found just the most perfect rock ever. Take turns explaining why your rock should be added to the family rock collection. Then have a family vote to select one rock. (Some families with plenty of space just let everyone bring their rock home.) Be sure to use a permanent marker to write the date and occasion directly on the rock. When you get home, find a permanent shelf or other place to display your rocks. Soon you'll have an entire history of family activities documented by rocks. It's fun looking at a rock and trying to identify where you found it, without peeking at the writing underneath!

197. Jiggling Pictures

Supplies: paper, pencil

After countless games of I Spy and License Plate Bingo, children might be ready for a silly game. Once again, plain old paper and pencil come to the rescue.

Give each child a piece of paper and marker or crayon. Explain that you'll ask them to draw a picture...but not in the normal way. Children place the papers on the top of their heads and draw the object with arms over their heads. Show the pictures afterward and see how many different versions of a dog or house are possible.

Now they place the paper on their chests and draw a picture without looking down. Again, you'll get some silly results. Can they contort their bodies and draw an item with the paper on their backs?

If the road is very bumpy, try holding a pencil very lightly on the paper. Watch it jiggle to make a picture of its own.

198. Beyond Paper and Pencil

Supplies: chalk, old socks, whiteboard and markers, "paint with water" coloring books, contact paper, construction paper, blunt scissors

Any car or plane trip requires a stash of paper and writing tools. Sometimes just the novelty of a new box of markers keeps children occupied making creative art pieces. Before your next trip, consider purchasing some of these items to help pass the hours:

■ Discount stores sell inexpensive chalkboards. Give children colored chalk to draw a picture and an old sock to erase their picture. If children get tired of drawing, they can use the chalkboard to play tic-tac-toe or hangman.

■ Whiteboards now come in small sizes. These easy-erase boards let children use special marking pens to draw vivid pictures. Once again, use an old sock to wipe the board clean.

■ Check out dollar stores for inexpensive "paint with water" coloring books. Each page has a paint strip of what looks like colored circles. Dip a paintbrush in a drop of water, touch the colored circle and you have paint to color the pictures. No mess other than a few damp pages in the coloring book.

■ Provide children with a piece of construction paper and strips of contact paper. Using blunt scissors, children can cut the contact paper into various shapes. After peeling off the backing, use the shapes to make pictures. If you feel uncomfortable using scissors in the car, simply hand children a bag of precut contact paper shapes. They can design pictures from the assorted shapes.

199. Catching the Giant Poontabuzz

Supplies: paper, pencil

You've sung songs, drawn countless pictures, and eaten all the junk food. Still the backseat gang seems restless and close to mutiny. If possible, take a short rest stop and then try this game when you're back on the road.

Prepare slips of paper, writing a "made-up" word on each. Ask children to help invent words such as:

- Baloonitist
- Zomeroni
- Baddlerkink
- Soonad Dustrimi
- Kapooler
- Providony

Often, children enjoy just creating a long list of words. Plus, spelling doesn't matter!

Give the first participant a slip of paper with a word on it. The object is to give a short speech, incorporating the made-up word flawlessly into the speech. Allow children thirty seconds to gather their thoughts. The results are very amusing as your child describes the importance of eating at least four troopalongas every day. After an enthusiastic round of applause, select another child to give a speech with another word no one has ever heard before.

200. Rest Stop Recreation

Supplies: jump ropes, squirt guns

"Mom! I can't wait! I have to go to the bathroom!" After hearing that, there's nothing more soothing to a parent's eyes than seeing the sign, "Rest Stop, Next Exit." Instead of using rest stops only for bathroom breaks, use the open space for some much-needed physical activity.

On your next visit to a rest stop, keep children moving with these ideas:

- ☺ Bring along jump ropes for each child. See who can jump the most times in one minute. You'll probably be approached by other parents complimenting you on the ingenuity of bringing jump ropes along!
- ☺ Have running races from one end of the rest area to another.
- ☺ When children beg for a snack from the vending machine, have them "earn" a treat by skipping around the outside of the restroom building at least five times.
- ☺ Bring out squirt guns and have a water fight on the lawn area—away from other people, of course!
- ☺ Find a grassy area for practicing cartwheels, somersaults, or hopping on one foot.

Whatever you do, take advantage of the open space before hopping back into the confines of a car.

201. Can You Imagine?

Supplies: paper, pencil

In an ideal world, children on trips would look out the window and say, "What lovely mountain scenery. Thank you, Mom, for bringing me along on this trip. I think I'll finish reading my book now." In reality, seatbelts get uncomfortable and siblings argue. This game brings some lightheartedness to backseat travel.

In advance, prepare slips of paper listing objects such as:

◆ A potholder
   A broken bus
   Shiny necklaces
   Wiggly worms
◆ A sick cat
◆ Cracked eggs
   A flat tire

On a different color paper, make a list of situations such as:

◆ Flying over a volcano
◆ Making a cherry pie
   Swinging on a hammock
   Going bungee jumping
   Riding a camel
   Spitting watermelon seeds

Take one slip of paper from each pile and combine the two topics in a story. Begin with the phrase, "Can you imagine if...a sick cat was riding a camel?" Then continue to make up a story, incorporating the two items. Keep the slips of paper because they can be reused to come up with different story possibilities.

202. The Power of Concentration

Supplies: any small items available, lapboard or stiff cardboard, paper, pencil

This is a standard party game that adapts easily to a car or plane. No advance preparation is required and you can use any items in your immediate vicinity.

Find a hard flat surface such as a lapboard or cardboard backing from a sketchpad. When children are not looking, place twenty items on the board. Use whatever is handy, from stale crackers to those bandages in your purse. Display items clearly on the board. Give children paper and pencil. Ask them to look at all the items for thirty seconds. Then remove the board. Children need to list as many items as they can remember. Compare their lists with the actual items.

For variety, play the game once as described above, then ask children to close their eyes. Rearrange the items on the board and remove two or three. Children open their eyes and try to guess which items are gone. Another sneaky variation is to display the board and have children stare intently at the objects. After they think they've memorized the items, have children close their eyes and ask them, "You stared at the items. But what am I wearing?" It's amazing how no one bothered to look at you because of the emphasis on the twenty items.

203. Same or Different

Supplies: paper, pencil

Children can gain an appreciation of cultural diversity by traveling. Even on a day trip, there's a good chance you'll run across food or customs that are different from your child's day-to-day world. Driving sixty miles from the casual-dress town of Bellingham, Washington, to the cosmopolitan town of Vancouver, British Columbia, reveals different accents and a much dressier clothing style.

Make a "Same or Different" chart to take on trips, listing numerous categories of things to see and do. Leave room to record similarities and differences in each category. Some categories could be:

- Foods
- Accents
- Clothing styles
- Style of houses and fences
- Design of street lamps
- Types of trees and flowers
- Species of animals
- Width of streets
- Number of buses
- Availability of subways
- Number of bicycles on the road

Keep the chart in a handy place. Throughout the day, when you see something different, jot it down. Be sure to note similarities on the chart also. Use it as an ongoing way to encourage children to be aware of their surroundings. One family from New York was shocked to visit a small town where the parking meter cost only twenty-five cents for two hours of parking. In some locations, McDonald's serves pizza. These little discoveries give new focus to your trip.

204. Goodies for Good Behavior

Supplies: small paper bags, stickers, markers, small gifts

Traveling long distances with children in a car usually ends up with parents offering bribes for good behavior. (Don't worry. All parents do it!) This activity encourages positive behavior without children realizing you are bribing them.

Before the trip, give each child five or six lunch bags. Some parents purchase colored bags to add a special "gift bag" feel. Let children decorate their bags with stickers and markers. Collect the decorated bags. When children are out of sight, place a small gift in each bag. Items could be:

- New markers
- Card games
- A jump rope or Frisbee for rest stop exercise
- Comic books
- A book of crossword puzzles
- Magic tricks to practice
- A special non-messy snack
- A coupon for a treat in the souvenir shop

Divide the mileage of your trip into equal amounts. If driving 600 miles, label each child's bag 50 miles, 100 miles, 150 miles, 200 miles, etc. Once the trip begins, have children check the odometer and figure out what it will read after 50 miles. When that mileage is reached, well-behaved children receive their 50-mile gift bag. Continue distributing bags at the designated mileage points.

Are We There Yet?

205. The ABCs of My Trip

Supplies: none

Coming home from a fun-filled trip can trigger a mild case of the blues. Wouldn't life be wonderful if we could live in a tent or go to waterslides every day? To help ease the transition back to school and chores, play this "I Remember" game.

Spend a few minutes discussing some experiences from the trip. What was the funniest thing that happened? What would you like to do again? What would you change about the trip? Where would you like to go on vacation next year?

Then take turns reminiscing alphabetically about the trip by saying, "When I went on my trip, I saw an Alligator at the reptile farm." The next person says, "When I went on my trip, I saw the Banana that Dad dropped during the picnic." Continue through the alphabet.

206. Terrific Travel Tips

Supplies: varies

A few practical travel hints can make a trip more enjoyable for everyone. The next time you are planning to travel, consider these ideas:

- ✿ If you have membership at the local zoo or science museum, see if your card entitles you to free admission in other states. Many museums and zoos offer reciprocal free or reduced admission.
- ✿ Take along plenty of sunscreen, film, and batteries that you've purchased at a local discount store. Hotel gift shops are notorious for high prices.
- ✿ If driving for long distances in the car, avoid eating at sit-down restaurants. Instead, find a school playground or park and let children run loose. If two adults are present, have one adult watch children while the other gets a picnic or fast food lunch. After children have played, continue driving and let children eat in the car.
- ✿ Consider staying in hostels when you travel. Many offer family rooms, complete with separate bathrooms. The price is low, and no one will notice if your children are noisy.
- ✿ When calling hotels to check prices, be bold and ask, "Is that the best rate you have?" Often they'll quote you a lower price.
- ✿ Avoid buying children new shoes for the trip. Nothing puts a damper on a trip to an amusement park faster than a child complaining because her new shoes are too stiff and giving her a blister.

207. Traveling with Terrific Toddlers

Supplies: varies

Older children can often be entertained on trips with their favorite magazines or card games. Since toddlers aren't quite up to a stimulating game of license plate bingo, other survival tactics are needed. If you are the fortunate parent of a toddler who immediately falls asleep in the car seat, rejoice! All other parents might find the following tips helpful:

☺ Bring along an inflatable ball. Toddlers love chasing the lightweight balls at rest areas or down hotel hallways.

☺ Pack a plastic spatula. Wrap the "flipping end" of the spatula with masking tape, sticky side out. Let your toddler hold the spatula when you go for a walk. He'll enjoy picking up tiny sticks or pinecones and attaching them to the tape.

☺ Include a few bottles of bubbles. Naturally your toddler will like running outside, trying to catch the bubbles. Be creative and blow bubbles in the car, letting children pop bubbles within reach of their car seats.

☺ If your child insists on using a particular type of spill-proof cup, purchase extra ones before the trip. Your favorite brand might not be available everywhere.

☺ If possible on car trips, occasionally sit in the backseat next to your toddler. Not only will it save your back from continually turning around, but your toddler will relish having you so close.

☺ Sheets of inexpensive stickers help pass the time. Toddlers can put stickers on paper bags, their clothes, and their hands.

☺ Toddlers love twisting and turning colorful pipe cleaners into interesting shapes. They are inexpensive and oh-so-quiet!

Natural Wonders

208. Marvelous Moth Milkshake

Supplies: tree, saucepan, stove, 1/2 cup sugar, 2 cups water, paintbrush or sponge, flashlight

Summer evenings are a great time to see fireflies, bats, and moths enjoying the warm evening air. You'll attract plenty of moths after making them this delicious drink.

In a saucepan, mix together the sugar and water. Have an adult stir the mixture over medium heat until the sugar is dissolved. While the mixture cools, find a paintbrush or sponge. When it starts to get dark, take your moth milkshake outside and spread it on a tree with the brush. Let the sweet liquid soak into the bark.

After an hour or so, take a flashlight and go out to the tree. You should have plenty of guests at your restaurant. If the moths are slow to find the tree, shine a light on it for several minutes. The combination of sugar and light is sure to make your tree a popular feeding spot.

Do you know how to tell a moth from a butterfly? When butterflies land on an object, they bring their wings up over their backs. Moths keep their wings separated.

209. Mini-Green Gardens

Supplies: plastic dishpan or flower pot, potting soil,
small pebbles, small shovel, seeds or small plants, water
Optional: acrylic paint and sealer, watering
can, spray bottle

Many parents with a love for gardening help children grow flowers and vegetables on large, weed-free plots of land. Those of us with brown thumbs are happy just to keep silk flowers from wilting. Find a middle ground by having your child grow a mini-garden.

To begin a container garden, you need...a container! Try a plastic dishpan, large flowerpot, or purchase a plastic window box. The size and shape doesn't matter as long as there is room to plant some seeds. Find a sunny location and you are ready to begin.

To add a personalized touch, have the children decorate the outside of the container with acrylic paint and then coat it with a waterproof sealer. This keeps the design bright after repeated watering. Provide the children with their own watering can or spray bottle.

Take your child to a home improvement store or a nursery to select seeds or small plants. Hardy flowers such as mums or pansies usually will survive a child's first gardening effort. Sprinkle small rocks on the bottom of the container for drainage. Add a few inches of good-quality potting soil. Plant the flowers, and for comparison, add a few carrot or radish seeds. Let your children watch the tiny, dry seeds emerging as green seedlings.

Gardening teaches children patience. In this age of instant gratification, children will wonder why their tiny carrot seeds don't instantly develop into Bugs Bunny–sized carrots. They'll also learn the responsibility of watering the plants on a regular basis. (Then, of course, there are those children who water enthusiastically and "drown" the plants.) If you have success with your dishpan garden, maybe you'll be inspired to plant an actual life-sized garden!

210. Crazy Letter Collection

Supplies: large wooden board, assorted twigs and roots, extra-strength glue

Don't expect to finish this activity in an hour...or even a weekend. Some families still haven't completed their display after six months! Don't let that scare you, because this is a low-key, ongoing project that can also involve friends and relatives.

The next time you are taking a walk or at the beach, develop a keen eye for twigs and roots. Your goal is to find small twigs, branches, or pieces of driftwood that naturally look like the letters of the alphabet. Of course, finding an *I* is easy, but just try to find an *R*! It can be done, though. Beech and maple trees produce gnarly branches and many exposed roots also have unique shapes.

After you've found a few wooden letters, glue them to a large wooden board. Be sure to leave room to add those hard-to-find letters. It won't be long until Grandma calls up to say, "Hey, I just found a *P*. Do you need it for your alphabet display?" Some families find themselves addicted to looking for letter shapes, even taking extra-long hikes in hope of finding that elusive twig that looks like a *B*.

Natural Wonders

211. Totally Terrific Trees

Supplies: trees, scarf or bandana for blindfold

Some people, when they walk through the woods or a park, simply glance at trees and assume that they are all alike. This activity helps children gain an awareness of details in nature.

Have your child pick out a tree. Spend five or ten minutes really looking at the tree and feeling the bark. Get acquainted with the smell, texture, and size of the tree. When your child feels satisfied she knows "her" tree, move about fifteen feet away. Blindfold her so she can't see.

Gently turn your child around three or four times so she is disoriented. Guide the child, still blindfolded, to a tree that is about the same size as "her" tree. As your child feels and smells it, can she guess if it is her tree? Move her to another tree and let her repeat the process. Finally, take her to her tree. Does she immediately recognize the tree by feel? Take off the blindfold and explain which trees she touched. Turn the tables and participate yourself. After examining a tree, let your child blindfold you and test your powers of observation.

212. Wooden Wonders

Supplies: branches or driftwood, paint, brushes

Have you ever walked through the woods and noticed an unusually shaped tree? Maybe the trunk was twisted or the branches looked like a witch's fingernails. Bring this concept home by finding wooden sticks and branches to create an assortment of wooden wonders.

Take a walk in a park or wooded area. Begin by noticing shapes and colors. What does that old stump remind you of? How many different colors of leaves can you find? As children become aware of different shapes, ask them to find two or three unique branches from the ground. If you happen to be at the beach, driftwood is perfect for this project.

When you get home, bring out the paints and turn an ordinary branch into a magical wooden wonder. Rub off any loose dirt or moss so you have a smooth surface. Does that long twig look like a wiggling worm? Maybe that driftwood shape could be turned into a butterfly with the addition of brightly colored paint.

Let the paint dry and display your whimsical wooden creatures.

213. Indoor Rainbows

Supplies: sunshine! shallow bowl or pie pan, water, small mirror

Everyone loves to see a rainbow arched across the sky after a rainstorm. Here's a chance to make your own rainbows inside the house. There's no guarantee you'll find a pot of gold at the end!

Try this activity on a sunny day. (It's pretty hard to get the rainbow effect without sunshine.) Place a shallow bowl of water in front of a sunny window. A pie pan or square baking dish also works. Give your child a small mirror that she can put halfway in the water without damaging the mirror. Let your child experiment getting just the right angle of catching the rays of the sun onto the mirror. Eventually, they'll find a way to get the "rainbow" reflection on the wall. (If you have dark-colored walls, tape up white paper so the colors show up better.)

Changing the angle of the mirror changes the color intensity. By reflecting the light on a nearby wall, you'll get a rainbow with distinct, intense colors. Shine the rainbow on a wall in the distance and it becomes larger, but the colors fade.

If you have several children, let them set up rainbow-making stations at different windows and flood the room with miniature rainbows.

214. Giant, Goofy Pumpkins

Supplies: soil, pumpkin seeds, heavy string or small rope, carving knife, plastic gallon milk jugs (translucent, not opaque)

Every October, magazines depict perfectly shaped, blemish-free pumpkins. Stores and vegetable stands display hundreds of pumpkins in a variety of sizes and shapes, most fairly round. With a little advance planning, your children can grow pumpkins unlike any sold commercially. Just remember to start this activity in early summer so your pumpkins have time to grow.

Purchase seeds specifically designed to grow large pumpkins (unless you want miniature jack-o-lanterns). Find a patch of soil that gets plenty of sun. Children love getting dirty as they work the soil, removing rocks and roots. Since pumpkins like lots of water, try to have a water source nearby. When the dirt is cultivated, form three or four mounds about the size of an angel food cake. Plant four to six pumpkin seeds in each mound (refer to seed packet instructions). Water well. After a few days, tiny seedlings should poke through the earth. Keep watering and soon the pumpkin vines will begin spreading down the mounds.

When the tiny pumpkins reach one to one and a half inches across, try a few experiments:

◆ Tie a small rope or string tightly around several pumpkins. As the pumpkins continue to grow, they will develop a figure-eight shape.
◆ Wrap string around two parts of the pumpkin and watch what shape develops.
◆ Measure your pumpkin weekly and record its growth.
◆ Take a picture of your child planting the tiny pumpkin seeds. Then photograph the pumpkin right before you pick it.

◆ When pumpkins are small and the skin is soft, help children carve their names into the skin. As the pumpkin grows, the letters grow also. You've just made a pumpkin tattoo!

◆ Clean several plastic gallon milk jugs thoroughly and lay them on the ground next to the pumpkins. Slip each tiny pumpkin inside the top of a milk jug. Mound dirt around the jug so it rests securely. After a few weeks, the pumpkins will no longer be able to slip out of the milk jugs. As they grow, their shapes conform to the shape of the milk jugs. When it's time to harvest, an adult can cut open the plastic bottle to reveal a Frankenstein-shaped pumpkin.

215. Butterfly Garden

Supplies: garden area, assorted flowers

Many children's museums and conservatories have butterfly gardens where people walk through an enclosed garden area, observing butterflies. It's amazing to see the look of wonder in a child's eyes when a beautiful butterfly lands lightly on her arm. With a little advance planning, you can create your own butterfly garden at home.

Begin in the spring, so plants have a chance to bloom and attract the butterflies. For best results, choose a sunny, sheltered area. Select plants from a local nursery or home-improvement store, or plant seeds according to package directions. Butterflies are drawn to large clumps of color, so plant flowers in several bunches rather than spread out. Butterflies especially like the nectar from these plants:

- Asters
- Black-eyed Susans
- Goldenrod
- Zinnias

Since butterflies start out as caterpillars, it's a good idea to have a section of untended weeds where caterpillars can munch away. They also like to eat cabbage, dill, broccoli, and asters. By setting aside a "caterpillar area," you'll be able to watch the beginnings of a butterfly garden right in your backyard.

Natural Wonders

265

216. Dress Up Nature Style, or "Adam and Eve Picnic"

Supplies: picnic supplies, glue, string, tape, knitting needle, leaves, moss, twigs, etc.

Some dress-up events require formal gowns and tuxedos. For your nature dress-up party, an elegant leaf necklace is more appropriate. Just watch out for the bugs.

Plan a family picnic in a park or other area where trees and shrubs are available. If you are leaving the backyard, bring along a few items such as glue, string, or tape to hold some clothing together and a knitting needle for poking holes.

Announce that family members need to dress in a very special way: a "natural" way. Give everyone time to collect an assortment of leaves, twigs, and pinecones. (Items should be found on the ground, not pulled from plants.) Use whatever tape or other odds and ends are available to fashion items to put over your own clothing. Have you ever felt a soft hat made of moss? What about an acorn wreath or a leaf necklace? When everyone is properly attired, eat your picnic in a natural setting, wearing natural accessories. Disregard the strange looks you get from people walking by.

217. Pretty Pressed Plants

Supplies: flowers, paper towels, heavy books
Optional: cardboard, glue, contact paper

Even if you find yourself artistically challenged, you'll enjoy pressing flowers. It takes very little skill and the results usually turn out looking professional.

To press plants and flowers you need...plants and flowers. Don't worry about depleting your flower garden. It only takes a few plants to get good results. Select small, flat flowers such as pansies or rose petals. (It's pretty hard to flatten a sunflower!) You can also take a nature walk and find wildflowers and interesting leaves or grasses along the way.

After you have an assortment of plants and flowers, lay them between absorbent paper such as paper towels. This helps soak up the small amount of moisture in each plant. Place several heavy books on top of the paper towels. Check the flowers after three to four days. When they are flat and dry, they are ready to use.

Pressed flowers make wonderful additions to note cards. Often, the colors remain bright. Gently glue the flower to the corner of a plain card. Brush a layer of glue over the whole flower to keep it intact. Or, arrange several dried flowers on cardboard and put them in a picture frame. Some people glue pressed flowers onto plain bookmarks. Cover with clear contact paper for durability.

Natural Wonders

218. From Bare to Hair

Supplies: plastic milk jug, sharp scissors, permanent markers, small rocks, dirt, water, grass seed
Optional: plastic wiggle eyes, felt, craft foam, glue

Instead of throwing your plastic milk jug in the recycling bin, use it to create a distinct personality with dirt and grass seed. Your character will quickly go from "bare" to "hair."

Wash the jug well with soapy water. Have an adult cut off the top portion of the milk jug, right below the handle, and recycle. The remaining bottom of the jug will become the face of your shaggy friend. Use permanent markers to draw on features. Glue on felt or craft foam eyes and mouth. Add extra-large wiggle eyes to create a longhaired, wide-eyed character.

Add small rocks in the bottom for drainage. Fill the jug with potting soil to within an inch of the top. Some people use a combination of peat moss and potting soil. One enterprising family incorporated the loose dirt thrown in piles on their lawn from a pesky gopher!

Sprinkle grass seed on top of the dirt. Press down firmly and add a light layer of soil on top. Water well and set in a sunny location. Be sure to mist the seeds daily to encourage growth. Within a week or two you'll see the "hair" start to sprout.

As the hair grows, add bows or cut the grass into a wild style. Keep watering for a long-lasting, green-haired friend.

219. Tabletop Lawn

Supplies: disposable aluminum casserole pan, potting soil, grass seed, mister spray bottle, water, plastic wrap

Ever envy your neighbor's luscious, weed-free lawn? Wish you could enjoy green grass without the hours of lawn work involved? Let your children show you how to have a no-hassle yard, right on the kitchen table.

For best results, use a disposable aluminum casserole pan, the larger the better. You could use your regular casserole dish if you don't mind not using it for several months. Fill the pan three-quarters full with potting soil. Sprinkle grass seed over the top and water with a mister spray bottle. Gently pat the seeds firmly in the dirt.

Create a mini-greenhouse by covering the soil with a layer of plastic wrap. Place in a sunny location. When you see the seeds beginning to grow, throw away the plastic. Let sunshine and fresh air help your lawn to grow. Within in a week, you'll have soft green grass growing.

To an adult, this is only a pan with grass in it. For children, the miniature lawn provides an area to set up a miniature soccer field, complete with action figure players. Another child might set up a golf course, or a scene with tiny dolls having a tea party. Keep the ground moist and leave the lawn on the table. It will be the basis for an ever-changing display.

Carry a Tune

220. Old-Time Music

Supplies: record player, paper plates, markers

Have your children ever seen a record player? You remember—those machines that played scratchy, vinyl records on a turntable? If you have an old record player in the attic, bring it down for modern-day fun and a display of creativity.

The first part of this activity is to explain how a record player works. Show your children what happens when you play a 45 record on 78 speed. (This alone will amuse them.) After they've laughed at the ancient technology and made you feel old in the process, bring out some white paper plates.

Poke a paper plate onto the record holder in the center of the record player. This keeps the plate in place. Set the record player to a slow 33 speed. Children hold a marker on the plate. As it spins, a design is created. Crank up the speed to 45 and then 78. Watch the spin-art designs create optical illusions.

Replace the plate when it's fully decorated. Children will enjoy experimenting with different colors, speeds, and techniques.

221. Making Musical Memories

Supplies: tape recorder, stereo or CD player,
musical tapes or CDs

We've all heard the saying, "Music soothes the savage breast." Try using music to settle down an excited child or to change the atmosphere of a stressful situation. Expand your children's repertoire beyond the latest teen sensation to include Beethoven or Johnny Cash (kids laugh at hearing "A Boy Named Sue").

Inexpensive tapes or CDs can be found at garage sales or checked out of the library. Incorporate music in the following ways:

- Take turns selecting background music to play at dinner. Each family member shares why they selected that particular piece. It's quite an experience to eat spaghetti with Zydeco music playing.
- Start some musical traditions. Wake up a birthday person with the Beatles' "Birthday." Play polka music while eating hot dogs or bratwurst.
- Play classical music and ask your children to draw a picture that fits the mood and tempo of the piece.
- Spend time simply listening and discussing "snippets" of music. Play a selection of bluegrass or a few Broadway show tunes. Ask the children for their comments on how the music makes them feel.
- If you need to have a serious talk with your child, try playing soft music in the background to create a calming atmosphere.
- Turn up the stereo with rock 'n' roll as everyone pitches in to clean the house.

222. Spontaneous Musical Merriment

Supplies: boxes, utensils, bottles, pot lids, etc.

In the olden days, families entertained guests in the parlor with violin or piano concerts. Ladies dressed in long skirts with elegant brooches listened attentively to the music. Men in dark suits smoked cigars and wished they were home. Today's families entertain with a more casual style.

The next time Grandma and Grandpa are coming over for dinner, plan to give them a concert that rivals Carnegie Hall. Instead of playing the violin or piano, make your own instruments. Send the family on a search throughout the house for homemade musical instruments. Some ideas are:

- Pound on a box with a wooden spoon.
- Rub your finger around the top of a water-filled crystal glass to make a high-pitched squeal.
- Hold a pair of tap shoes and hit the soles on a cookie sheet.
- Fill an empty plastic bottle with unpopped popcorn. Seal the top and shake.
- Put on a pair of ski gloves and clap your hands together.
- Bang two pot lids together. (This is very popular.)

When the guests arrive, play a song with your unusual instruments. See if anyone can guess the name of the song. Try singing a song while playing instruments. It's difficult to sing anything when the person next to you thinks he's playing an instrument by banging an empty paper towel tube on his head.

223. Old-Fashioned Sing-Along

Supplies: paper, pencils, song sheets, refreshments

It's hard to believe that, in the days before television, families actually entertained themselves by singing together. Revive this ancient activity by inviting friends and neighbors over for an old-fashioned sing-along.

Have children make handwritten invitations to carry out the old-fashioned theme. Invite people to bring any instruments they may have stashed away in the attic. It's fun asking people to come dressed in *Little House on the Prairie* clothes. Don't worry about fancy refreshments. Serve popcorn and sassafras or root beer.

As singers arrive, hand out song sheets with words to familiar songs such as *Bicycle Built for Two* or *In the Good Old Summertime.* If possible, find an outgoing person to lead the singing. Enthusiasm is more important than the ability to carry a tune. For variety, let your children lip sync to a popular song from today. The emphasis, however, should be on singing songs from days long gone by.

224. Modified Wheels on the Bus

Supplies: paper and pencil

Any bus driver transporting a group of preschoolers has heard them sing, "The Wheels on the Bus Go Round and Round...." Older children enjoy singing this song also, especially when they get to make loud horn sounds and yell, "Move on back!" If you know the familiar tune, you can adapt the words to your particular trip.

Give older children pencil and paper and ask them to write new lyrics before sharing them with everyone. This not only takes more time, but it helps them organize their thoughts. Younger children can make up new verses by shouting out their ideas.

How about singing a song that begins with:

☺ The wheels on the dirty van go...
☺ The Mom in the car says, "You're in time-out..."
☺ The juice in the cup spills on the floor...
☺ The kids in the SUV just want to get out...
☺ The baby in the car needs his diaper changed...

Children will develop a variety of verses geared to your specific trip. So go ahead and plan the debut of your new song...soon to be released on CD!

225. Wacky Words

Supplies: paper, pencil

Going over the river and through the woods to Grandma's? After singing "Ninety-nine Bottles of Beer on the Wall" for the tenth time, channel your children's lyrical abilities by writing their own songs.

Begin by singing a few popular songs everyone knows, like "Jingle Bells" or "Row, Row, Row Your Boat." Then give children paper and pencil to use for writing "Wacky Words" to the familiar tunes. How about:

(Sung to the tune of "Row, Row, Row Your Boat")
Drive, drive, drive your car,
quickly down the lane
Jason has wet his pants and
Dad's going insane

Children have the uncanny knack of taking ordinary travel situations and making them funny through the adapted songs. If your family isn't musically inclined, work together on rewriting "'Twas the Night Before Christmas." It might begin like this:

'Twas the night before vacation and everywhere you could look,
Mom and Dad stacked clothes, toys, and even some books.
The suitcases were packed by the front door with care,
But Dad lost his keys and began pulling his hair.

Don't worry about the correct iambic pentameter!

Being Your Best

226. Do We Really Need All This Stuff?

Supplies: copy of the book **Material World**
by Peter Menzel

Your children probably complain about not having enough toys, clothes, or computer games. As a dutiful parent, you tell them to be thankful because children in other parts of the world don't have basic necessities. Your children nod in agreement, but still secretly wish for more "things."

The next time your children have the "gimmes," try this activity to put their wants in perspective. Gather the family and briefly discuss their favorite toys or special items. What items do they need and what items do they simply like to have? Give them ten to fifteen minutes to go through the house and pick ten items that are most important to them and bring them to the living room. (If Dad feels the refrigerator is important to him, have him jot "refrigerator" on a piece of paper and bring that instead of the actual refrigerator.)

After the items are collected and you have a cluttered living room, discuss why the items are important. Bring out the book *Material World* by Peter Menzel. Look at the pictures together and be prepared to answer probing questions. The book depicts families from around the world in front of their homes. Each gorgeous two-page spread shows a typical family from the country, their home, plus all of their belongings. Compare a typical American split-level with stereos, bikes, microwaves, dressers, and closets of clothes to an African family's home and belongings. Children will see a picture of a mud hut and the entire family's possessions consisting of a few blankets, two chickens, and a few pots.

The book is an eye-opener about how we live in comparison to the rest of the world. Keep the book handy. You'll find children going back to look at it over and over again.

Being Your Best

227. Soothing Stress Reducer

Supplies: two small, heavy latex balloons; birdseed; scissors; large funnel

Many gift shops carry pliable stress-reliever balls. You roll or squeeze them, supposedly releasing your stress by playing with the balls. Instead of paying gift shop prices, have children make their own stress balls.

Blow up a balloon and release the air several times to stretch it. Try to use a heavy-duty latex balloon rather than the thin, water-balloon type. Place the neck of a funnel inside the balloon. Fill the balloon with as much birdseed as possible. Keep pressing down the birdseed to get a solid feel throughout the balloon, except for the neck. Remove the funnel and tie a knot in the balloon. Cut off the extra latex above the knot.

Carefully cut off the neck of the other unfilled balloon. This is the protective layer that fits over the birdseed balloon. Stretch the unfilled balloon over the first balloon. Make sure the two balloon openings are opposite each other.

It's surprising what a unique feeling the birdseed creates as you squeeze the ball or roll it around on your skin. You'll find yourself taking the stress reliever away from your children so you can play with it.

228. Blind Trust Walk

Supplies: scarves or bandanas for blindfolds, two or more people

Back in the crazy sixties, this blind trust walk was a popular activity at group gatherings. Partners would lead each other around, saying, "Wow, this is really cool, man." Then they'd bump into things and still say, "Wow, this is really cool, man."

Relive your youth by experiencing the trust walk with your children. Begin by putting a scarf over their eyes. (Very young children may not want to participate in this activity. If that's the case, let them lead you around.) Explain that you'll simply lead them through the house or outdoors. This is not a trick event where you try to knock their heads or make them bump into walls. Start slowly, letting your child hold onto your arm. Make small comments such as, "We need to turn left now," and, "Take a small step down." After a few minutes, ask if your child knows which room he is in. Can he tell if you led him outside?

Switch places and let children lead you around. Be careful if you have a prankster in your family. She may get you to walk into a wall! After everyone has a chance to be the leader or follower, ask a few questions. What was it like to have to trust the other person? Would you rather be a leader or a follower? How did you feel when you took off the blindfold?

229. Discover Your Community

Supplies: form of transportation

Most families travel in a familiar "loop." We drive a certain route to school, the soccer field, and our favorite grocery store. Yet who knows what you'll find on a hidden side street? Encourage a sense of discovery as your family seeks out unique specialty stores or businesses.

The next time you drive by the oriental grocery store, make a point of going inside. Yes, it might be awkward, but you'll probably find a friendly store clerk eager to help. A great conversation starter is: "Hi. We often drive by your store, and finally decided to stop in. Do you mind if we look around?" Appoint children to spot businesses new to the family. Take them to an actual shoe-repair shop. Yes, there are still people around who have shoes repaired instead of simply buying another pair! Visit a bonsai nursery or a shop selling gold-mining equipment. You don't have to buy anything. You do need to show children that people in their community have a variety of interests and special talents.

Ever wonder what goes on behind the scenes at a radio station? Give them a call and see if you can visit. Visit a fire station or exotic pet shop. One mother went so far as to make an appointment to bring her children to a prosthetic company. They watched in amazement as skilled workers fashioned artificial hands and legs. Not your typical Saturday afternoon in the park, but it certainly provided something to talk about on the drive home.

230. Secret Good Deeds

Supplies: varies

As parents, we want our children to grow up as responsible citizens. Part of that involves developing compassion for other people. Help children learn how to help others by performing secret good deeds together.

Children love surprises and secrets. Tell them that you plan to do a good deed for someone. Select a neighbor, friend, or relative. Brainstorm what type of secret deed your family could do to make that person happy. Some ideas are:

◆ Mow an elderly neighbor's lawn when she's gone. Sweep her sidewalks, etc. Part of the fun is peeking out the window and watching her face when she comes home and sees a manicured lawn.

◆ Go to a pick-your-own berry field and pick fresh strawberries for a friend. The effort of picking conveys more concern than buying berries at the store. Put the bowl or basket at the front door, ring the doorbell, and run!

◆ If a friend or neighbor needs cheering up, make a few signs that say, "You're special!" or, "We're here to help." Place the signs in the bushes around the person's house.

◆ Make a giant card for Grandma, covered with drawings and pictures…just to tell her you love her. Mail it without a return address. She'll figure out who it's from.

By performing "secret" good deeds, children have the excitement of trying to keep from being discovered, but also gain awareness of other people's needs.

231. Low-Cost Cultural Awareness

Supplies: local newspaper

Do your children only listen to pop music? Would you like to get beyond watching concerts on television? With a little effort and just as little money, children can be exposed to the performing arts. Local community productions give children an awareness of life beyond the current teen heartthrob.

Check the local newspaper for listings of upcoming events. You may already attend puppet shows or sing-along concerts. It's easy to skip over announcements about student concerts or college symphonies. Here are some ways to make children's "grown-up" cultural experiences positive:

- Discuss in detail what to expect. Explain how a play is different from a video. Role-play how to sit quietly and applaud when appropriate. Above all else, no kicking the seat in front of you!
- If going to see a performance of a popular event such as *The Nutcracker,* read a book about the plot ahead of time. Children are more attentive if they understand the storyline.
- Don't feel you have to take children to Carnegie Hall for a live performance. Begin by attending the orchestra concert at a local school. The atmosphere is more relaxed and children still have a chance to experience a concert.
- With younger children, leave at intermission if they get restless. It's more important to have a positive experience than sit through the second half with antsy children.
- In the summer, look for outdoor concerts. Children have the freedom to move around while discovering the world of the performing arts.

232. Thought for the Day

Supplies: chalkboard or white board with markers

As parents, we have good intentions to impart profound words of wisdom to our children. In reality, we spend most of the time saying mundane things like, "Pick up your dirty socks," and, "How many times do I have to tell you to stop teasing your little brother?" You can call on the recorded wisdom of famous people to broaden your child's understanding of the world.

Select a chalkboard or whiteboard that can be displayed in an easy-to-see location. Find a book or website listing quotations. (If you're clever and productive, you can use your own wise thoughts and quote yourself.) Every few days, copy a quote on the board. Have some of them be controversial. Casually ask children what it means, and why they think the person made the statement. Do they agree or disagree with the quote? A few examples might be:

- "Work hard, be yourself, and have fun!"
  —Michelle Kwan
- Challenges can be stepping stones or stumbling blocks. It depends how you view them.
- "When you play, play hard. When you work, don't play at all." —Theodore Roosevelt
- A man without a goal is like a ship without a rudder.

Older children might enjoy finding their own quotes and displaying them. Ask your child why he chose that specific quote. Have children write down profound sayings they made up on their own.

233. What Would You Do?

Supplies: index cards, pencil

Most children have pat answers about how they would handle awkward situations. "What do you say if someone offers you drugs?" "I'd walk away." "What should you say when Aunt Edna gives you an ugly hand-knit sweater for your birthday?" "Thank you, Aunt Edna. It was nice of you to give me a gift." Use this game to help children develop ideas for some wacky situations.

On a set of index cards, ask children to list various locations. One card might read "in the supermarket" or "in a wading pool". On another set of cards, list serious and lighthearted situations, such as:

- ✿ Your friends dare you to steal a candy bar.
- ✿ Your sister asks for help with homework.
- ✿ You burp (loudly) while standing in front of the class to give a book report.
- ✿ Your pet cockroach eats your homework.

Each person selects a location card and a situation card. Put the two together and share what you would do. You'll end up with silly situations like, "You are in a crowded elevator and you have to sing 'Take Me out to the Ballgame' as loudly as you can. What do you do?"

Children gain confidence thinking how to creatively solve real and imaginary situations.

234. What's So Good about That?

Supplies: none

We often tell our children there are two sides to every situation. Chocolate chip cookies taste great, but fifteen cookies in a row could cause a bit of discomfort. This game helps children look at ordinary situations from different perspectives.

Ask your children a simple question such as, "What is good about broccoli?" They'll tell you it's healthy, grocery stores make money when they sell it, etc. Then ask, "What's bad about broccoli?" You might get answers such as its bad taste or how it could interfere with breathing if you stuck it up your nose.

Present a number of subjects and encourage children to see the positive and negative aspects. You could ask:

- ☺ What are some good things that happen because we have stop signs? What are some bad things that happen because we have stop signs?
- ☺ List positive and negative aspects of long fingernails.
- ☺ List positive and negative aspects of tattoos.
- ☺ List positive and negative aspects of owning a computer.
- ☺ What are good and bad reasons to own a kangaroo?
- ☺ What are the positive characteristics of your parents? (No need to ask for negative characteristics!)

235. Work-at-Home Opportunities

Supplies: paper, pencil

"Mom, I want a new CD."

"Hey Dad, can I have some money to play miniature golf with Zach?"

In spite of all our well-intentioned lectures on the importance of saving and spending money wisely, children constantly "need" cash. Here's a practical way to show them that money really doesn't grow on trees. Instead of lecturing, set up a JOBS AVAILABLE list.

In a conspicuous place, display a list of work-for-hire opportunities. Children can pick and choose from the list to earn additional spending money. (These are jobs beyond their regular household chores.)

Some examples are:

◆ Roll all the loose change into paper coin holders.
◆ Organize the kitchen pantry.
◆ Sweep the garage.
◆ Sort boxes of family pictures.
◆ Dust all the windowsills.
◆ Clean the doghouse.
◆ Wash out the recycling bins.

Assign a monetary amount to each task and make sure jobs are age-appropriate for each child. The next time children clamor for extra money, they can get it the old-fashioned way...they can earn it!

236. Giant Trash Monster

Supplies: large piece of butcher paper or cardboard, markers, small plastic bowl, glue, paintbrush, water, litter!

Here's a semi-sneaky way to get a large group of children to help clean up after a birthday party or activity at the park. It's especially effective for scouting groups that need to leave the area spotless after an overnight camping trip.

Get a large piece of butcher paper, at least eight feet long. An even better alternative is to use the large flattened cardboard from an empty appliance box. On your drawing surface, sketch out the shape of a "monster." Don't worry about your artistic ability. Anything with a fierce scowl and large body qualifies as a monster.

Explain to the group that your monster is naked. (This alone causes laughter.) Their job is to give the monster "litter fur" by collecting any pieces of paper, balloons, gum wrappers, soda cans, etc. Ask for volunteers to spread glue all over the monster's body. To make this easier, pour a bottle of glue into a plastic container and add a few teaspoons of water to dilute it. Use a paintbrush to cover the monster with glue.

At the designated signal, children race out to find any pieces of litter on the ground. (If you are in a wide-open space, be sure to state the boundary areas so no one gets lost in their enthusiasm to find the perfect piece of trash.) As children find litter, they run back and glue it on the monster. It won't be long until your monster is fully "dressed" and the surrounding area spotless. Now it's your job to dispose of the litter-covered cardboard monster!

Budding Artist Games

237. Budding and Blooming Artists

Supplies: paper, watercolors, brushes,
large shirts for artist smocks
Optional: easels, music

Ever wish you could escape from day-to-day life by sitting at an easel next to a stream in the French countryside? In silence, you'd paint the château off in the distance while sipping local wine. In reality, you're busy cleaning up the mess your children made finger-painting on the kitchen table. If you can't visit the French countryside, at least have children experience outdoor art at its finest.

Set up an outdoor art studio. Painting outside lends itself to a whole new feeling. If you have an easel, bring it outside. Children can also paint on picnic tables or thumbtack paper to a fence. Provide plenty of watercolors or paint for each child. Even if the children are wearing play clothes, have them wear a painting smock. Any large shirt put on backward gives that true artist look. Berets are optional.

Ask your children to paint the landscape around them. At first, you'll get traditional paintings of trees and the neighbor's doghouse. Then give out fresh paper and start the music. Just turn up the stereo from inside the house or bring out a portable tape player. Try a variety of music, ranging from classical to the Beatles, while children paint according to their feelings. Compare the "paint-by-music" paintings to the landscape pictures. Which ones use more color? Which express more fluid motions? Maybe you could sell your child's modernistic painting for enough money to finance a trip to France.

238. Priceless Stained Glass

Supplies: powdered tempera paint, dishwashing soap, small containers, paint brushes, paint smocks, newspaper

Feeling really brave? This activity sounds messy, but with a little planning in advance you'll find yourself with colorful windows and very happy children.

Since you want the paint to be thicker than normal, use powdered tempera paint. This lets you mix it to the gel-like consistency you need. Mix several colors of paint with water in empty yogurt or margarine containers. Here's the key to easy clean-up: after the paint is mixed with water, add one or two teaspoons liquid dishwashing soap. When it's time to remove the dried paint from your window, the soap helps loosen the paint.

Set out paintbrushes, cotton swabs, and sponges. Be sure to cover the windowsill and surrounding floor with newspaper. Paint smocks are a good idea, also. The paint should be thick enough to stay on the paintbrushes and not drip all over the floor. Let your budding artists get to work painting a window or sliding glass door. They'll enjoy painting abstract scenes or even self-portraits.

After the glass paintings have been on display for a time, use a wet rag to wipe the windows clean. The combination of tempera paint and soap makes for quick clean-up. Just when you get your windows sparkling clean, you'll probably hear, "Can we paint them again?"

239. Mystery Rubbings

Supplies: crayons, paper

As children get more comfortable in the high-tech world, they miss out on low-tech, high-touch experiences. This simple activity gives children the chance to feel and smell a variety of objects. You can't do that with a computer.

Bring out a handful of crayon stubs from the bottom of the toy box. Peel off all of the paper wrappings. Show your children how to take a rubbing by laying a piece of paper over a coin and rubbing the flat side of a crayon over it. If a child has never done this, they are amazed to see the coin's image transferred to the paper.

Give each child paper and a crayon. Ask them to go on a "mystery hunt" and take rubbings from items inside or outside the house. Children stay happily occupied trying to find objects to rub. Every time they rub an object, a different texture appears, so the activity is always new. When everyone is done, have them come back and show off all of the rubbings. Try to guess what item created each image. Often, the children rubbed so many objects that they can't remember themselves if the rubbing is from the carpet or a smooth tree bark.

Budding Artist Games

240. Magic Marble Roll

Supplies: tennis ball container, paper, acrylic paint, small bowls, spoon, marble

Some parents have the ability to plan complicated, detailed craft projects. Their children sit quietly for hours, making intricate wax designs on authentic Ukrainian eggs. If your children would rather throw eggs than decorate them, here's a simple craft project for you.

Give each child an empty tennis ball or Pringles potato chip container. (This avoids having to take turns.) Let your children figure out how to cut a piece of white paper to fit completely inside the tube, overlapping slightly. Set up two or three small containers with different colors of paint. Use a spoon to drop a marble in one color of paint. Use the spoon to retrieve the paint-covered marble and plop it inside the tennis ball container. Put the lid on and start spinning! Children can shake, rattle, and roll the container as long as they want.

Remove the marble and repeat the process with another color of paint. When completed, carefully remove the paper and let dry. You have a very modern art/abstract painting! It can be used as wrapping paper for small gifts or as the background for greeting cards. Your children will probably want to decorate many pieces of paper because they enjoy the shaking process.

241. Easy Stained-Glass Displays

Supplies: clear contact paper, tape, colorful paper or tissue scraps, leaves, yarn pieces, etc.

You know you should give your children the opportunity to express their creativity through arts and crafts projects. Yet when the supply list includes gold-leaf spray, designer-oil pastels, and embossing guns, you know you are in over your head. Instead of searching all over town for exotic craft supplies, bring out the tissue paper and contact paper.

Cut your child a piece of clear contact paper. Place it on a flat surface, sticky side up. To help keep the work surface in one place, tape the corners down. Bring out an assortment of paper scraps, leaves, or yarn pieces. Tissue paper, construction paper, or even pages from old magazines work well.

Have your children cut or tear sheets of paper into various shapes. Place the shapes directly on the sticky contact paper to create a picture. When complete, carefully cover with another piece of contact paper, putting sticky sides together. Press firmly and trim the edges. Hang in a window for a no-fuss stained glass display.

Budding Artist Games

242. Extra-Long Pictures

Supplies: rolls of adding machine paper, markers, crayons
Optional: adding machine

Sometimes an ordinary item allows children the chance to be creative. A small roll of adding-machine paper provides the basis for yards and yards of drawings.

If possible, show your children how an adding machine works. They'll enjoy adding a string of numbers or challenging you to beat the machine at basic math facts. If a machine isn't available, just provide the roll of paper. Many garage sales sell rolls for less than a quarter each.

Find a smooth drawing surface such as a hardwood or tile floor. Set out markers or crayons and have children draw pictures. It's fun to write a very long letter to someone. Perhaps they want to make a border for their bedroom walls. One budding mathematician used the long roll to write out the mathematical equation for "pi" as far as he could: 3.14159265358979323846264433, etc.!

243. Crazy Characters Picture

Supplies: paper, markers

Most children have no qualms about drawing pictures. It's adults that feel they have no artistic talent. Here's a drawing activity that is so wacky, it doesn't matter if you only draw stick figures.

Hand everyone paper and a pencil or marker. The youngest family member begins by stating the name of any object, such as "a spotted kangaroo." Everyone draws a spotted kangaroo. The second youngest person calls out another object, such as "a broken teacup." Now you need to draw a broken teacup so it somehow "interacts" with that famous spotted kangaroo. Maybe the teacup is balanced on the kangaroo's head. Take turns adding silly items to the picture.

After you've drawn six or seven objects, compare pictures. See how people used the same items but produced entirely different compositions.

Water
Fun

244. Wacky Water Fun

Supplies: sprinklers, hoses, resealable plastic sandwich bags, squirt bottles

Water fun is certainly refreshing on a hot day, but sometimes children need a few inspiring ideas for how to keep cool. Here are ways to have fun in the sun:

- When children get tired of simply jumping over a sprinkler, reverse the process. Have an adult attach the sprinkler on the sturdy branch of a tree. The water creates a different effect by sprinkling *down* on children.
- Attach a hose to the top of the slide on the swing set to create a water slide. Caution children never to stand up while on a wet slide.
- Remember the game of "high water, low water," using a jump rope? Two people hold the rope taut while others try to jump over as the rope gets raised higher and higher. Play the same game with one person holding a hose that has the type of nozzle that creates a long, thin stream of water. Children jump over the water line, trying not to get wet.
- Give children clean spray bottles and let them spray each other. For safety, insist that they use the "mist" setting, instead of the solid water stream.
- Water balloons are difficult for children to fill and tie. Instead, give them resealable sandwich-sized plastic bags. Children can toss them to each other and get soaked if the bag breaks open. Best of all, you can use the bags over and over.

245. Wet and Wild Piñatas

Supplies: large, heavy-duty balloons; plastic grocery bags; broomstick

A traditional piñata carries all the elements of fun: excitement, skill, and candy! Instead of having a one-time-use piñata, try these water-filled balloon piñatas on a hot day.

Get children to help you blow up some large, heavy-duty balloons. This helps stretch them. Let the air out and refill them with water. Try to get the balloon as large as possible. Tie the end. (Usually by this point the balloon has either popped or sprayed water all over you, but keep persevering.)

After you have several heavy water balloons, place each balloon in a plastic grocery bag. Attach the bag to a tree branch or the top of a swing set. Begin the game just like a regular version of piñata: blindfold a child and hand them a stick. Spin them several times and then urge them to try and bat the bag filled with the water balloon.

It's quite obvious when they've made contact. Instead of candy, they get sprayed with water!

246. Giant Ice Cube Rides

Supplies: grassy hill, giant blocks of ice, small towels

The next time your children are bored on a hot day, tell them, "Go ride an ice cube!" They'll question your sanity, so go ahead and show them how it's done.

Purchase several large blocks of ice from the local convenience store. Stick them in the trunk and take the kids to the nearest grassy hill. By this time they will really be wondering what you are up to.

Take the blocks of ice to the top of the hill. Remove the plastic bags and cover the top of each block with a towel or dishcloth. This prevents small legs from getting freezer burn. Ask an enthusiastic volunteer to sit on the giant ice cube and slide down the hill. Watch out, you can really pick up speed! Since children are so low to the ground, there is little danger of getting hurt if someone falls off. Younger children may need help maneuvering the chunk of ice back up the hill.

If you have several ice blocks, try racing down the hill, side by side. Children can keep sliding for several hours as the cubes get smaller and smaller.

Water Fun

247. Spontaneous Car Wash

Supplies: dirty cars, buckets, rags, sponges, mild detergent

Do your children complain that they never have enough money? Are they trying to earn money for a new bike? Instead of setting up a traditional lemonade stand, help them make big bucks by offering a "Spontaneous Car Wash."

This activity works best in a neighborhood where you know most of the neighbors. For safety reasons, an adult should be present. Collect in a wagon or plastic storage container all the supplies you need to wash a car: buckets, rags, sponges, and mild detergent.

Here's where you begin your spontaneous car wash. Go to a neighbor's house and announce, "Hello. We're offering a spontaneous car wash. If you bring out your hose, we'll supply everything else—including labor—to wash your car for the low price of $_____." Most people are so impressed with such a clever way to earn money that they gladly haul out the hose and let you wash their car. When done, simply collect the money and move on to the next house.

Now, if you can only get your children to wash your own car!

248. Acrobatic Alligator Wrestling

Supplies: swimming pool or lake, inflatable alligator, aquarium glue or other watertight glue, Velcro

Most children have seen television shows where fearless thrill-seekers attempt to wrestle alligators. The explorer stealthily sneaks toward an unsuspecting alligator and grabs his snout, trying to avoid becoming the alligator's lunch, as we watch the action from the safety of our living rooms.

This activity requires you to purchase a live alligator at least six feet long. If your local pet shop is out of alligators, try buying a plastic inflatable one. Blow up the swamp creature so it is firm but still flexible. Using aquarium glue, attach a piece of Velcro about 2" x 2" on the nose of the alligator and the opposite Velcro piece on the tail. Let the glue dry thoroughly.

Now get ready for some wet and wild alligator wrestling! Ask for a volunteer to "wrestle" the alligator. Toss the alligator in the pool. If your children can swim, they go in the deep end of the pool and try to connect the two pieces of Velcro. This means they attempt to attach the tail to the nose. It's quite comical to watch kids flip around as they try to get the alligator to cooperate. Make sure there's adult supervision for this activity (you don't want the alligator getting the upper hand!). If several children are participating, time each one to see who is the fastest alligator wrangler. For younger children, let them wrestle the alligator while standing in the water, rather than floating.

249. Homemade Underwater Viewer

Supplies: plastic gallon milk jug, sharp cutting tool, plastic wrap, rubber bands or duct tape, markers

Going to the lake or beach? Since children are fascinated with water, let them make their own underwater viewer to observe underwater animal life. They may not see colorful fish and coral like at the Great Barrier Reef, but they may see tadpoles, plants, bugs, or seaweed.

Have children thoroughly wash out a plastic gallon milk jug. An adult should cut off the bottom inch of the jug and recycle it. Children can decorate their viewer with permanent markers.

Spread a piece of clear plastic wrap over the cut end of the jug. Attach it with thick rubber bands or duct tape to form a tight seal. Your underwater viewer is complete! Children can put the viewer in the water while squinting their eye over the mouth of the jug. The plastic wrap actually provides a slight magnification, so chances are that children will see some bugs or plants underwater.

250. Surprise Water Balloon Volleyball

Supplies: large flat playing area, assortment of balloons, water, two buckets or boxes, old sheet or shower curtain, clothesline or swingset

Traditional games of volleyball require teamwork and skill. Surprise water balloon volleyball requires only a willingness to get sopping wet on a hot day.

Help children fill twenty to thirty balloons with water and tie them shut. Fill a variety of shapes and sizes, ranging from flimsy water balloons to sturdy twelve-inch party balloons. Divide your group into two teams and divide the water balloons equally between them. Give each team a bucket or box to store their stash of balloons. Instead of a regular net, you'll need an old sheet or shower curtain to help add to the element of surprise. Drape the sheet over a clothesline or swing set, high enough to block one team from the other's view. Don't worry about the net being regulation height. The rules of water volleyball are very relaxed!

Have the teams spread out on either side of your sheet/net. Begin like a volleyball game by having one person serve the "ball" over the net. The opposite team tries to gently catch the water-filled balloon and either lob it over the net or pass it to another team member. As you can imagine, many balloons break upon impact or splatter to the ground. It's extra-exciting because children never know for sure when a balloon will appear from over the net.

Have plenty of balloons handy for the game and extra towels for wet volleyball players.

Safety tip: Pieces of latex balloons are very dangerous around young children, who can choke on them. If preschoolers or toddlers are in the area, pick up and dispose of any popped balloons immediately.

251. Wet Parent Relay

Supplies: large flat playing area, plastic pop bottles, permanent marker, paper cups, buckets of water, chairs

As an adult, you probably enjoy quiet, educational games where there is little chance of discomfort. This family activity is neither quiet nor educational and there's a strong chance you'll get wet. Your children will think this is the greatest game ever invented.

Select four to six adults who sit innocently on chairs at the finish line. Use a permanent marker to draw a line directly around the mid-point of plastic two-liter soda bottles, one for each adult. This is the water line that needs to be reached. Have each adult hold a bottle between his or her knees.

Children line up, relay race style, with each line facing an adult. Each team has a bucket of cold water by the starting line. (Some groups throw a few ice cubes into each bucket to make sure parents really suffer.) On "GO!" the first child in each row takes a paper cup, dips it into the water and races down to their adult. Giddy with excitement, they try to pour the water from their cup into the soda bottle. Naturally, half goes onto the adult's legs. Then they run back and pass their cup to the next runner, who repeats the process. The winning team is whichever fills the bottle to the marked line first.

Some groups have the adults hold the bottles between their upper thighs. Then of course, when the game is over, the adults have wet pants, causing great delight among the children.

252. Wet and Wild Relay Race

Supplies: large flat playing area, buckets
of water, plastic containers
Optional: obstacles like pillows or wading pool

Children enjoy participating in relay races more than actually determining a winner or loser. It's enough fun to race and cheer for your team members. For an extra element of fun, just add water.

Line children up, typical relay race style. Have the start and finish lines twenty to twenty-five feet apart. Put a bucket of water at the beginning of each team's starting line and empty buckets at the finish line. Give a plastic margarine or yogurt container to the first person in each line. On "Go!" they fill the small container with water from their bucket. Then they must put the water-filled container on their heads and try to get to the finish line without spilling it. No hands allowed! When they get to the finish line, they dump the water (if there's any left!) and race back to their teams, where the next person fills the container and puts it on his or her head.

Add a twist to the race by setting up a simple obstacle course where children have to run around a plastic wading pool or step over a pillow. If younger children have trouble balancing the cup, give them a water-soaked sponge to put on their head.

Water Fun

253. Super Water-Ball

Supplies: large flat playing area, spray bottles
or giant water guns (such as Super Soaker),
towels or boxes for goals, beach ball

Combine a hot summer day and children with water to create a perfect setting for fun. To play Super Water-Ball, every child needs a spray bottle or a "super-duper" water gun. If you don't have enough, ask the children ahead of time to bring their own.

Divide the playing area in half. Set up a goal in each end zone using boxes or a beach towel. Split the children into two equal teams. Line the teams up, facing each other in the center of the playing field. Drop a beach ball between the teams and watch the action begin. The children try to squirt the ball to their goal, while the other team is frantically squirting the ball in the opposite direction. First team that gets the ball to their goal wins that round. Be sure to allow time to refill all those water bottles!

A variation on this game is to set up two simple obstacle courses with a few chairs or potted plants. Line children up in two equal lines, relay race style. On "Go!" the first person on each team squirts the beach ball around and through the obstacles. When they get back to the starting line, hand over the water bottles to the next person and start directing the beach ball through the course again. Have an adult ready to hand off filled squirt bottles or squirt guns so children don't lose time refilling their water squirter.

254. Fantastic Forts

*Supplies: swing set or trees for support,
old king-size sheets, rope
Optional: pillows, rugs, etc.*

We've all seen pictures of incredibly detailed children's forts. Some millionaire parent hires an architect to build his child a backyard fort complete with two stories, a drawbridge and moat, and a built-in sound system.

If that seems a bit too elaborate for you, help your children make a one-of-a-kind fort using everyday materials. After all, children usually play in a fort for a few days and then lose interest as they take up skateboarding or other activities.

Using several sheets makes one of the easiest forts. Check out garage sales for inexpensive queen- or king-size sheets. Help your children find a sturdy support for the fort. If the structure is sound, the children can decorate and personalize the fort without worrying that it will fall apart. Try draping several king-size sheets over a swingset. This gives children enough room to stand up in. If you want a cozier fort, string a rope between two trees and hang the sheets over the rope. Use rocks for weights, or let your children figure out on their own how to make the sides spread out to give more room.

After the basic structure is complete, let your children search for ways to decorate their fort. An old carpet on the floor adds comfort, along with pillows or low chairs. Add a few cartons or shelves to store books, flashlights, or food, and you have a great fort for hours of imaginative play.

If You Build It...

255. Incredible Paper Structures

Supplies: paper, tape, objects of different weights, such as sponge, book, etc.

Most people look at a piece of paper as something flimsy to write on. With some tape and creativity, paper becomes a tool to use for building structures. This is also a great way to use scrap paper from the recycling box.

Provide an assortment of paper of different shapes and sizes. Spend a few minutes showing children how to fanfold paper to increase its strength. Rolling paper into tubes and then taping edges also forms a strong shape.

Ask your children to make any kind of structure by taping pieces of tubes or fanned paper together. Make the task more complicated by saying, "Here's a sponge. Can you make a structure that supports the sponge?" After they succeed with that task, give them a heavier item like a book. See if they can figure out how to bend or fold the paper to make something strong enough to hold a heavy object. They'll surprise themselves at seeing how simple pieces of paper can support a book or toy.

256. Big, Beautiful Boxes

Supplies: large cardboard appliance boxes,
paints or markers, sharp cutting tool
Optional: beanbags, sponges

You don't need to buy a new refrigerator for this activity. You do need to track down a cardboard refrigerator box for hours of fun. Many appliance stores crush appliance boxes, so it's a good idea to call and ask them to save you one.

Once you've managed to wrestle the box into your backyard, find and remove any large packing staples sticking in the cardboard. After the safety check, let your children loose. Other than having an adult cut windows, children can paint and decorate on their own. Here are some fun uses for appliance boxes:

- Pretend the box is a submarine. Add pipes for a periscope and draw round windows on the side. As your children pretend to go under the sea, sneak up to the submarine with a glass of water, toss it inside and yell, "Your sub is sinking!"
- Stand the box upright. Cut a large window on one side and use it as a ticket booth for pretend games of circus or carnival.
- Cut several various-sized holes in one side of the box. Give a point value to each hole such as five, ten, or fifteen. Toss beanbags or small balls in the holes and see who gets the highest score.
- Make a Pie-in-the-Face or Wet-Sponge booth. Stand the box upright. Cut one hole so a person's face peeks out. Someone gets in the box and sticks their face out of the hole. Other friendly folk toss whipped-cream pies or wet sponges gently at the exposed face.
- Let children connect boxes with secret passageways like in an old house. How about bringing sleeping bags and camping out in the boxes?

257. Super Space Station

Supplies: large cardboard appliance box, aluminum foil, duct tape, glue, permanent markers
Optional: pie plates, juice can lids, aluminum pans, paper fasteners (brads), dryer vent hose

Sometimes bigger truly is better. Children like making miniature scenes in shoe boxes; why not increase the scale and expand the fun? Give budding astronauts an appliance box and watch them build a space station that rivals NASA.

The key to a successful space station is ample aluminum foil. Buy the cheapest foil and let your children glue and wrap the foil around the entire box. This creates an instant spacy feel. Silver duct tape around the edges provides an even more realistic effect. (Astronauts use duct tape in outer space, don't they?)

With the basic silver base complete, let children look around the house for items that move, wiggle, or turn. Use paper fasteners to attach paper plates as small steering wheels. Glue on silver juice can lids as space sensors. Poke hoses or a section of a dryer vent through the cardboard for a semi-realistic space control arm. Any type of aluminum pan looks like it belongs on a silver space station. Use permanent markers to draw numbers and fancy words on the control panel.

Store the space station in a dry location. Children enjoy adding and deleting items on an ongoing basis. You never know when you'll find that perfect spray nozzle to attach to a space station!

258. Tooth Fairy Hotel

Supplies: box, assorted craft supplies, matchbox
Optional: small doll furniture

Remember the last time you played tooth fairy? You probably sneaked into your child's bedroom at night and tried to find their itty-bitty tooth somewhere underneath a crumpled pillow. You kept searching, hoping your child wouldn't wake up to see you stealing her tooth. Solve the problem by creating a splendid Tooth Fairy Hotel with a special place of honor for a tooth.

Since children love going along with fantasy, tell them the tooth fairy travels so much from house to house, sometimes she needs to rest in a hotel. Provide a box and assorted craft supplies so children can build their own five-star hotel. Use tissues for bed blankets and toothpaste caps for light shades. Children will search the house looking for items to use in their miniature hotel. When a child loses a tooth, bring out the hotel and place it by her bed. Often they'll want to add to their work-in-progress by making new curtains or adding flower boxes.

Most important: decorate a small slide-out matchbox or other tiny box with silver glitter as the special tooth holder. This precious box sits in a place of honor in the hotel. It's much easier to remove a tooth from a matchbox than digging under a pillow!

259. Rube Goldberg Contraption

Supplies: household items such as tubes, boxes, toy cars, tape, etc.

Ever wonder what went through Rube Goldberg's mind? He's the man that developed all sorts of comical, complicated contraptions. He created a machine to crack an egg. Instead of rapping the egg against a sharp edge, he got more involved. When you go to get your morning paper, a string opens the door, which then pulls a lever that knocks a ball that hits a glass, which falls and knocks over a monkey sitting in a chair. The monkey jumps up and steps on the egg, cracking it. Get the picture? Rube Goldberg became famous for his clever but impractical inventions.

Inspire your children to new heights of creativity by letting them design their own Rube Goldberg machine. Find a picture of a Rube Goldberg invention on the Internet or an encyclopedia. This will help children visualize the chain-reaction type of machine they should build.

Give a simple task, such as the previously mentioned invention to crack an egg. Perhaps they could design a machine to push the "on" button on the remote control. How about a machine that pushes a rocking chair? After giving children a basic task, set them free to use anything they find (within reason) to make the machine. Depending on their interest, this could take several hours.

After the machine is complete, play a drum roll and set the machine in action. Even if it doesn't work perfectly, take a picture or video to document this one-of-a-kind machine.

260. Cozy Creature Houses

Supplies: boxes, paper, glue, scissors, fabric scraps

They sit on beds, fall under desks, and collect dust everywhere. Yet what would childhood be without an abundance of stuffed animals? The only thing missing for most fuzzy dogs and bears is a decent place to live.

Ask your children if they've ever considered making homes for their favorite stuffed animals. Bring out empty boxes, fabric scraps, and markers. Let them create a variety of habitats. How about a diorama with jungle plants for a stuffed parrot? Or a cozy igloo for Perry the Penguin? Sew or glue fabric together for a soft dog bed. Just looking at each animal will spark your children's imagination about how to make a home. Make sure each home has a nice sign, such as "Lamby's Lovely Barn."

If You Build It...

261. Moo-velous Building Blocks

Supplies: rectangular paper milk cartons, dishwashing soap, water, scissors

Instead of buying children expensive wooden blocks, try making your own. Children enjoy building with these sturdy (and free) blocks. The more milk they drink, the more blocks they have to play with.

All it takes is some half-gallon milk cartons. You will need two cartons per block. Use rectangular paper cartons rather than plastic milk jugs. Wash the milk cartons thoroughly in soapy warm water. If you like, add a drop or two of bleach to the final rinse solution to disinfect and deodorize.

When milk cartons are clean and dry, have an adult cut off the top two or three inches where the pouring spout is located. You want a plain rectangle with a straight edge at the top. For each pair of cartons, make a slit on each corner of the open end of one of the cartons, going down about three inches. Hold one carton in each hand, open ends facing each other. Slide one carton inside the other. Push firmly together. The two cartons form an extra-sturdy block. Continue with the rest of the cartons, making more and more blocks. Once you've used up all the cartons, use your new blocks to build amazing structures. If a block does get crushed, just drink more milk and make more blocks. Best of all, these blocks can be left outside since they are durable and waterproof.

Use **Your**
Imagination

262. The Fairy Godmother Says...

Supplies: Something to use as a magic wand

Ever wish you had a fairy godmother? Now you can at least act like a fairy godmother (or godfather) and actually have some control over your children. To get the full effect from this activity, it's *very* important that you have a magic wand. (If you really want to get extra points, find something frilly to wear as a fairy godmother dress, complete with a tiara.) Even if you are artistically challenged, you can cover a stick or wooden spoon with aluminum foil and tell your children that it's the latest in wands.

Explain to your children that this wand has magical powers. If you tap someone with the wand, they immediately have to do what you say. In your very best fairy godmother voice, tap a child (lightly!) and gave a command such as, "Poof! You are a shark, swimming in the ocean." Your child proceeds to give her best impression of a shark. Vary the activities by saying, "Poof! You are a famous gymnast and must stand on your head." Children enjoy acting out the mini-scenarios. Gear the activity to the space available to you. Some parents get creative and actually succeed in saying something educational such as, "Poof! You now will count to 50 by 5s." Other scenarios could be:

- ☼ A child building a snowman
- ☼ A bee buzzing from flower to flower
- ☼ A racecar driver whose car goes out of control
- ☼ A teacher trying to control an unruly class
- ☼ A child picking up his toys (Hey! It's worth a try!)

If you have more than one child, send the extra child out of the room while you say the "spell." When she returns, have her try to guess what the first child is doing.

263. Fantasy Architecture

Supplies: old magazines, glue, scissors,
cardboard or manila file folder

"Mom, can I paint my bedroom?"

"Why do I have to share a room with Jessica?"

"Can I get new curtains and a bedspread?"

Even if your children's rooms have toys, computers, and shelves of books, they probably want something else. The next time your children ask to make major changes to their rooms, let them. Tell them they can do anything they want to redecorate their room. Money is no object! Then hand them a stack of magazines and tell them to design a fantasy bedroom.

Along with the magazines, give your children a large piece of cardboard. Manila file folders can provide a basis for their project also. Tell them that they can cut out items from the magazines, designing their dream bedroom as if money were no object. The only other supplies needed are scissors and glue.

Join the fun and design your own dream kitchen or family room. Cut out pictures from the magazine and glue them to your cardboard. Decide how to arrange furniture and where to put the hot tub. Children will enjoy sitting next to you, commenting on a piece of furniture or equipment they found. After all, doesn't everyone have a swimming pool and trampoline in their bedroom?

After the architectural collages are complete, take time to have each person share her room and explain why they chose the layout she did. The fact remains, even if you did provide your child with her dream bedroom, there would still be dirty socks on the floor!

264. Imagination City

Supplies: solid-color shower curtain,
permanent markers

Use Your Imagination

Fabric stores sell preprinted panels with mock layouts of cities. The fabric has bold colors with streets, fire stations, and houses. Children lie on the floor with toy cars to pretend they're driving through town.

Instead of buying a town with perfectly drawn-out streets, let your children make their own. Set out a solid-color shower curtain on the floor (you can find an inexpensive one at a discount store). Provide permanent markers and watch the young architects design their ideal town. They'll enjoy making railroad tracks running along a river. Maybe they'll design a new mall.

This activity is a work in progress. Some children draw the basic streets and then spend the rest of the time adding toy cars or small dolls. Other children play for a few minutes and then get the urge to add a bakery or draw window boxes on the houses. Simply leave the markers nearby and children can embellish their town as much as they want. When play is done, fold up the town-on-a-shower-curtain and store it in a closet until next time.

265. Whatcha' Doing?

Supplies: three or more people

Some children have incredible coordination and concentration. It's easy for them to rub their stomachs and pat their heads at the same time. Here's a game designed to help children develop an awareness of what they say and do.

Have one child pantomime a simple action, such as brushing their teeth. The game proceeds like this:

- ☺ Child No. 1 pretends to brush her teeth.
- ☺ Child No. 2 comes up and asks, "Whatcha' doing?"
- ☺ Child No. 1 keeps brushing her teeth, but answers by saying something different from what she is actually doing. Perhaps she says, "I'm digging a hole."
- ☺ Child No. 2 takes over and pantomimes digging a hole until he's asked, "Whatcha' doing?" by another player.
- ☺ Child No. 2 says, "I'm doing somersaults."
- ☺ The next child begins doing somersaults and the game continues.

It's hard to believe how difficult it is to do one action while saying that you're doing another. Children easily get mixed up and have to concentrate.

266. Weekend Resort at Home

Supplies: complete house and yard

The glossy brochures from family resorts inspire armchair travelers everywhere. They offer fantastic food, supervised children's programs, and daily housekeeping services. They even provide a parent's night out so Mom and Dad have time alone. When you look at the price sheet, however, reality sets in. If you can't afford a five-star resort, get creative and enjoy a luxury stay in the comfort of your own home. Here are some tips to make your stay-at-home weekend a success:

◆ Set aside a weekend specifically for your family's mini-vacation. If something comes up, simply say, "We'd love to come to Jordan's party, but our family is spending the weekend at the Johnson Family Lodge."

◆ Use your answering machine! Vow not to run to the phone every time it rings. The purpose of the weekend is to spend time together, not chatting on the phone.

◆ Sit down with the family ahead of time and let each family member select an activity. Even though you'll pay to go bowling or swimming, the cost is much less than at one of those deluxe family resorts.

◆ Try to see your community through the eyes of a tourist. Are there pick-your-own strawberry fields nearby? How about visiting the museum at the local college? Take advantage of an all-you-can-eat pancake breakfast offered by the senior center. Do something unusual like participating in a family road run/walk. Just participating in new experiences makes you feel like you're on vacation.

- Go ahead and bring out the junk food (in moderation, of course). Ride bikes to the local bakery on Saturday morning and enjoy warm doughnuts. Eat hot fudge sundaes while watching a family video. Spending time together is more important than a healthy diet for the weekend.
- Buy a new game ahead of time and play it over the weekend.
- Keep cooking to a minimum. Tuna fish sandwiches served on paper plates make a fine meal when accompanied by a purchased cheesecake.
- End the weekend by scheduling another family resort weekend for six to eight months later.

267. Pup Tent Party

Supplies: small, free-standing tent; sleeping bags

Sometimes all children need is a new "prop" to produce hours of fun. What better prop than a pup tent in your living room? Don't panic—if you can get access to a stand-alone tent you won't have to drive tent stakes into your living-room carpet.

On a rainy weekend when bedtime isn't as important, ask your children if they'd like to camp out in the living room. The hardest part of this activity is searching the garage to find where you stored the tent, or asking a neighbor to borrow theirs.

Once you have a tent, set it up, bring out the sleeping bags, and let the children pretend to be on a camping trip. Many children entertain themselves rearranging sleeping bags or even reading inside the tent. If you are going for "Parent of the Year," serve hot chocolate and offer to tell mild ghost stories.

After everyone is settled in the tent, head off to bed and let young campers giggle themselves to sleep.

268. Fantasy Vacation

Supplies: map or globe, reference materials

Getting ready for a month-long tour of Europe next summer? Looking forward to a 'round-the-world cruise on your own private yacht? Or do you plan on visiting Grandma and camping in a state park? Most families only dream of visiting exotic (and high-cost) destinations. If you can't actually pack your suitcases and hit the road, try planning a fantasy vacation.

Get out a globe or world map. Select a family member to close his eyes and randomly point to a spot on the map. His finger determines where you'll spend your fantasy vacation. Yes, you may end up in Siberia, but at least it's only a fantasy!

Use the Internet or library to get information about the location. What is the climate like? How much does it cost to get there? What language do they speak? Take a trip together to a travel agency and ask for brochures. Even if you end up exploring an "ordinary" location like Pittsburgh or Arizona, you'll still gain experience in planning a trip. On the other hand, you may find yourself researching an imaginary trip through the rain forests of Costa Rica. You might even find out that traveling to an unusual destination is possible with planning and a few money-making garage sales.

269. Challenging Chindogu

Supplies: assortment of household items

The next time you have group of children together, get them involved in Chindogu. What's Chindogu? No, it's not a form of sushi, but an activity designed to encourage creativity. Chindogu, which originated in Japan, is the fantastic world of useless inventions. There is actually an organization with ten thousand members from all around the world.

Some real Chindogu inventions include:

- Fuzzy slippers for cats so they can help dust as they walk through the house.
- A complete face shield to protect your hair from any broth that might fly up as you slurp noodles.
- Plastic cups attached to each shoulder to catch your earrings in case they fall off.
- Fish eye covers. Who wants to see the glazed stare of a fish as you get ready to fillet him?
- A toilet paper dispenser that attaches to your head, so you always have paper available to blow your nose when you have a cold.

With those ideas for inspiration, divide into groups. Give each group an assortment of odds and ends found around the house. Ask them to create a working but totally useless invention. After a designated time, have each group demonstrate what they created. You'll be amazed.

270. Secret Lives of Apartment Dwellers

Supplies: paper, markers or crayons

Have you ever taken a walk and casually peeked into someone's window? It's fun to see different furniture or wall decorations as you glance into their private lives. In Holland, people frequently leave their living room curtains open, even in the evening. Their philosophy is, "We live honest lives and have nothing to hide. Why should we close the drapes?" Here's a way to peek into windows without getting into trouble.

Before a trip, make a sketch of an apartment building. Artistic ability isn't important—simply draw a tall building with six to eight large windows. Label each window with an apartment number like 3C or 2A. You'll need a copy for each child. Once you're on the road, ask children to look into the windows of homes or stores you pass. What do they see? Are children playing? Are stores closing for the day? Give each child a copy of the apartment house you've drawn, and crayons or markers to draw a scene in each window. What's happening in apartment 6B? Can they see a baby crib or a dog looking out the window?

After the scenes are finished, call out an apartment number such as 7C. Each child describes what they drew for that particular apartment.

271. Did You Really Do That?

Supplies: none

As a responsible parent, you've taught your children never to lie. "Honesty is the best policy," you've told them. Here's a game that encourages falsehoods...but it's all in fun.

Ask a child or adult to share three things about themselves that are true, and one that is false. You might hear something like this from your ten-year-old:

- I learned how to tie a square knot at camp last week.
- I pinched my sister yesterday in the hotel.
- My best friend is Jacob.
- The last book I read was a *Hardy Boys* novel.

Other family members try to guess which is the false statement. It's not as easy as it looks!

Children love to have adults play also. They'll find out all your hidden secrets like the time you snuck into the men's dorm at college in the days of same-sex dormitories.

272. Going to Antarctica

Supplies: none

When you are traveling, hopefully you have a final destination in mind. During the process of getting where you want to go—or any time you are looking for instant entertainment—play this game that could inspire you to travel to new locations.

The object is to state where you are going and what silly thing you will do there. The locations and reasons need to be in alphabetical order. Made-up, fantasy destinations are encouraged! For example:

- ☼ I'm going to Antarctica because I want to eat ants.
- ☼ I'm going to Belize to see some dancing bananas.
- ☼ I'm going to Catooga to plant cantaloupe.
- ☼ I'm going to Denmark to pick daisies.

Take turns among family members to state where they are going and the reason for their trip. You thought you were taking a normal visit to see Grandma, but your daughter is planning to go to Switzerland to collect swizzle sticks!

273. Solve the Mystery

Supplies: small suitcase or backpack, assorted items of clothing, ordinary household items
Optional: paper and pencil

This simple activity works great on trips or any time you want to get the family together. The idea is to announce that you found a mysterious suitcase and the family is to play detective and discover who the owner of the suitcase is. (For best results, be as dramatic as possible.)

When no one is looking, gather five or six unrelated items and put them in a small suitcase or collapsible backpack that your family hasn't seen before. The backpack might contain a pair of old pants, a plastic bag, a coffee filter, a roll of tape, a spatula, and a wrinkled newspaper. At an opportune moment, produce the bag with a great flourish, announcing that you have found a mystery suitcase. If you're travelling, you can slip the suitcase to the hotel bellman and ask him to deliver it to your room with instructions to find the owner. Your children will be truly impressed.

With older children, ask them to write down a description of the person who owned the suitcase and why he/she carried those items along. They'll eagerly write graphic descriptions about a man who likes to sneak into restaurants at night, steal coffee filters, and make pancakes using his own spatula. Each description ends up being unique. Younger children can simply tell you about the suitcase's owner. Some families use this suitcase game as an ongoing trip activity, with different family members changing the contents of the suitcase daily.

special
Occasions

274. Family Award Night

Supplies: paper, ribbons, glue, scissors, markers
Optional: candles, flowers, tiny white lights,
red carpet or construction paper

Even the best of families have times when angry words are spoken and bickering takes place. Try to focus on the brighter side of your family's interactions. Designate an award night to celebrate all the positive aspects of family life that often go unrecognized.

Ahead of time, vote on a favorite meal. (More than likely you'll end up ordering pizza.) Make up a variety of award certificates complete with ribbons for every family member, such as:

- ☺ Best Sense of Humor
- ☺ Kindest to Animals
- ☺ Best at Doing Chores
- ☺ Easiest to Make Giggle
- ☺ Most Willing to Help a Friend

Even though the meal itself is casual, encourage everyone to dress up for the event. Yes, put on those fancy clothes you wore to the last wedding (panty hose are optional!). Set the table with candles and fresh flowers. String tiny white lights around the entrance to the dining room.

Try to find a red carpet. Otherwise, just tape pieces of red construction paper to the floor. Have children enter the room one at a time. As they parade down the red carpet, light the way with a flashlight and pretend it's a floodlight similar to the Academy Awards.

After everyone is seated and eating their favorite meal, begin announcing the awards. Read them in a dramatic voice and have the winners give an acceptance speech. You'll all leave the meal with a positive outlook toward each other.

Special Occasions

275. Breakfast Picnic at the Park

Supplies: picnic basket with muffins, juice, etc.

It's a lazy weekend morning when everyone can sleep in. No alarm clocks, no rushing to catch the school bus. Take advantage of the relaxed morning by having a breakfast picnic at a local park. No need to drive far. Pick the closest park with playground equipment and prepare for early-morning family togetherness.

Pack a picnic basket loaded with breakfast goodies: muffins, juice, fresh fruit, or bagels. Add coffee in a thermos and the newspaper for adults. You'll actually have time to read the paper while children play on the playground. Some families bring sausages and barbecue on the park grill. You could even find your camping frying pan and make pancakes. No matter what you serve, it will taste delicious in the early-morning fresh air.

Surprise your children and invite another family to join you for breakfast. Parents can chat as the kids use the uncrowded playground equipment. Exercise, good fun, and time together...sure beats watching cartoons!

276. Home-Sweet-Home Dinner

Supplies: typical dinner supplies, balloons, paper, markers

Can't afford taking the family to a five-star restaurant? Tired of eating at fast-food establishments? Then make reservations at a restaurant where the price is right and you can freely kiss the staff!

In the afternoon, announce to your family that the dining room is scheduled to be transformed into a restaurant for the evening meal. Assign jobs to make the transformation possible. This could include:

◆ Decorating committee to add atmosphere. Include signs, menus, and a theme.
◆ Serving staff with uniforms and skill in pouring milk and serving meals.
◆ Chefs to make the meal *magnifique!*
◆ Clean-up crew for the ever-popular jobs of washing dishes and putting away leftovers. (This group earns an extra-late bedtime.)

Everyone works at his or her task until mealtime. Even if the chefs simply serve spaghetti, the meal takes on a new perspective with Italian background music and hand-drawn gingham tablecloths. It's fun to have waiters at your beck and call. You might consider leaving them a tip! Show your children that spending time together is more important than eating off white linen tablecloths in a stuffy restaurant.

277. Waldo's Wild Party

Supplies: balloons, streamers, party hats and horns
Optional: fabric paint, permanent markers,
pet leash, pet bowl

During a recent informal survey, Americans revealed that the majority of households celebrate their pet's birthday. If you've never throw a wild bash for Fluffy and Rufus, you don't know the fun you're missing. (Don't worry if you don't know the actual birthdate of your pet goldfish. Pick any date to celebrate.)

Children love parties of any kind, so they'll be thrilled when you announce it's time to celebrate the dog's birthday. Let children decorate with all the traditional balloons and streamers. Buy a new pet dish and have children decorate it with permanent markers or acrylic paint. Be sure to wrap it up so it is an official gift. How about purchasing a new collar and leash? Children can decorate the leash with fabric paint for a one-of-a-kind gift.

On the day of the big event, prepare a special meal for the pet of honor. One family cooked their pet hedgehog "extra-lean" ground beef instead of the cheaper variety. Sing a rousing chorus of "Happy Birthday to Simba" and don't forget to take a picture of your pet wearing a goofy pointed party hat. Unless he's a goldfish, of course.

278. Happy Half-Birthday Party

Supplies: cake, cards, balloons, party supplies, etc.

Waiting a whole year for another birthday seems like an eternity to a child. Break up the twelve-month wait by celebrating their half-birthday. Find the date six months from your child's birthday and get ready for a family celebration.

The silliness of this event makes up for the lack of fancy presents. Try some of these ideas:

- Blow balloons up halfway so they hang limply on the wall.
- Cut paper plates and napkins in half. (Note: Paper cups cut in half get rather messy.)
- Serve half a birthday cake that says "HAP BIRT" in frosting.
- Sing the ever-popular Happy Birthday song, only stop singing halfway through.
- Give half a present, such as the top to a jogging suit. (The pants can mysteriously appear a few days later.)
- Cover half of each present in wrapping paper and cut the bows in half.
- Play Pin the Tail on the Key (Half of "Donkey." Get it?)
- Let the birthday child stay up half an hour later than her usual bedtime.

279. Good Vibrations Cake

Supplies: cake, narrow ribbon, foil, paper, pencil

Serving a cake at a meal creates an instant feeling of "fun." The next time you have a cake, turn it into an instrument for conveying positive messages.

Ask everyone to write what he or she likes best about their family on a small piece of paper. Roll the paper into a small tube and cover with aluminum foil. Tightly attach a twelve-inch ribbon to the message.

If you are extra ambitious, make a cake from scratch. Otherwise, buy a cake from the grocery store. Let your children carefully poke the foil-wrapped messages into the cake, leaving the ribbon hanging out. When you're ready, cut pieces by slicing between the ribbons and serve.

As people eat their cake, unwrap the messages and share them with the rest of the family. The compliments give extra flavor to the cake. This activity works for birthday celebrations, also. Have everyone write short notes saying positive things about the birthday child. Insert the notes into the cake.

280. Do-It-Yourself Decorating

Supplies: party decorations, e.g. balloons, streamers, etc.

You're planning a party for ten enthusiastic twelve-year-olds, and still have to bake cupcakes, blow up balloons, and plan games. The dog throws up and your schedule gets pushed back even more. Don't worry. Simply turn some party preparations over to the guests.

As guests arrive, hand each child a few streamers and balloons. Tell them, "Everyone is in charge of decorating for Jennifer's party. Get to work!" (Some parents encourage the decorating to take place outside, away from breakable items.) You'll be amazed at how excited children get to decorate. They'll laugh as they blow up a balloon and lose all the air while trying to tie the end. It's preteen humor to wrap crepe paper streamers around the barbeque. Everyone needs balloons attached to her toilet.

Instead of hiring a professional cake decorator, let guests decorate their own cupcakes. Set out frosting, knives, sprinkles, and small candies. Children will happily entertain themselves, smearing gobs of frosting on a single cupcake, laughing the whole time. Isn't that what parties are all about? Now if you can just get them to help with clean-up....

281. Your Very Special Day

Supplies: varies

Think of how your child feels on his birthday. It's a glorious day filled with special food, presents, and lots of attention. On a child's birthday she probably can get away with not taking a bath or adhering to normal bedtime. Of course, parents are exhausted from organizing all the events! Help your children relive a scaled-back version of their birthday by designating one day during the year as "Their Very Special Day."

Pick a date when life is halfway predicable and no major holidays are approaching. Explain to your child that he gets to choose meals and activities (within reason, of course!). A few ideas are:

- Serve your child breakfast in bed.
- Include a special treat in their school lunch box.
- Give a few wrapped gifts such as colorful socks or shiny new pencils.
- Let your child select the evening meal...with dessert first if they want!
- Pick your child's favorite activity to do after dinner.
- Have other family members make a card describing the special child's skills and talents.

Include parents in this activity. Children learn to reciprocate by planning special treats for Mom or Dad on their special day.

282. Giant Moving Greeting Card

Supplies: garage door, streamers, balloons, paper, markers, duct or masking tape

If it's Susie's birthday or Grandma is coming for a visit, it's natural to decorate with balloons and streamers. Putting up signs with personalized greetings makes anyone feel special. With only a small amount of effort, you can create a gigantic moving billboard right in your own home.

Stand inside your garage and close the large door. Warning! Make sure your car is out of the garage before making your display! Blow up and tie an assortment of balloons. Tear crepe-paper streamers into various lengths. Using duct or masking tape, attach the streamers to the bottom edge of your garage door. Tape the balloons to various sections of the streamers. If you have a large sign that reads "Welcome Home, Kevin!" or "Happy Birthday, Alison!" tape it securely to the bottom of the garage door, also.

Are you beginning to see what you're creating? When the big moment comes and your special guest pulls up in the driveway, you open the garage door. As the door slowly rises, it reveals streamers, balloons, and signs. Drive through the lightweight decorations and pretend you're going through a multicolored car wash.

283. Celebrate National Twinkie Day

Supplies: Twinkies
Optional: paper bag, brooms, beige
clothing, strawberries

In the everyday routine of homework, chores, and work, it's easy to get bogged down with the seriousness of life. Here are activities guaranteed to make your entire family smile.

It's hard to believe, but April 6 is actually National Twinkie Day. (You can probably celebrate any day of the year, though.) Begin the celebration by purchasing several boxes of Twinkies. Then try these activities:

- ✿ Serve Twinkies and milk for breakfast! Twinkies have about the same nutritional value as regular sugary cereals, so don't worry. Your kids will remember this for a long time.
- ✿ Play Twinkie Piñata. Fill a paper bag with Twinkies (still wrapped). Play a game of hitting the piñata to get the Twinkies inside.
- ✿ Organize a game of Twinkie Broom Hockey. Set up two goals in the garage or driveway. Family members play a modified version of broom hockey using frozen Twinkies for pucks.
- ✿ Try a Twinkie toss. Have your children select a partner and toss Twinkies (still wrapped) back and forth like an egg toss. Best of all, if a Twinkie is dropped, it still can be eaten. Don't try that in an egg toss!
- ✿ Tell everyone they have to dress for dinner in beige to look like a Twinkie.
- ✿ Serve a delicious dessert to those dressed in their beige Twinkie costumes. Slice Twinkies horizontally and cover with strawberries for Twinkie Shortcake.

284. Special Interest Nights

Supplies: varies

Some parents, highly skilled in organization, easily arrange neighborhood day camps or special interest programs for large groups of children. If you're the less-structured type, get together with friends occasionally for special interest family nights. Here's how:

☺ Gather five or six families together who enjoy being around each other.

☺ Select a regular meeting date and time such as the first Tuesday of every month from 6:30–8:00 P.M.

☺ Rotate the host families. On your designated night, have your family provide planned activities for everyone. This could mean playing charades, going on a scavenger hunt, or making homemade ice cream. The other families simply show up, knowing their turn to host is coming up in several months.

☺ Try to involve all family members in the planning process. Delegate children to decorate and even clean up. They'll enjoy participating, knowing they have a stake in the success of the evening.

☺ Don't feel you have to meet often. If five families are involved, meet every other month. That way each family plays host only once a year.

285. Children's Toy Swap

Supplies: paper and pens (or computer) for flyers
or posters, tables, tokens (tickets, poker chips,
or Popsicle sticks), excess toys

Wondering what to do with all those old toys your kids never use anymore? Try a kid's toy swap. To be successful, recruit at least twenty participants—this provides everyone with a greater selection of toys to exchange.

Begin by having your children help you design a flyer stating the date, time, and location. Ask participants to bring up to ten gently used toys or games to exchange. Stress that everything should be clean and in good repair. Smaller items, such as action figures or doll clothes, could be bundled together to make one item.

Here are some guidelines:

◆ Children drop off their toys at a designated location and time.
◆ For each item donated, the child receives a token of some kind in exchange.
◆ After children drop off their toys, have an adult entertain the children while you sort the toys into sections.
◆ Place books in one area, games in another, etc. This makes the event more like shopping in a real store.
◆ Open the doors and let the shopping spree begin! Children select toys and pay for them with their tokens. A child who brings eight toys will have the chance to exchange them for eight "new" toys.

This is a popular event since "one child's trash is another child's treasure." They'll go home with new-to-them toys and parents haven't had to pay any money. That's a great shopping spree!

286. Trick or Trunk!

Supplies: Large parking lot with good lighting, cars, candy, carnival type prizes and decorations

Many communities hesitate to encourage children to go door-to-door on Halloween. Often, schools and community groups plan alternative activities such as carnivals to help children celebrate in safety. You don't have to build bulky carnival booths; use the trunks of cars for hassle-free trick-or-treating.

Select a school or church parking lot that can be blocked off so that cars are not driving through once the event begins. Adults park their cars in designated spaces—most groups form a large circle, similar to a wagon train round-up, with all the car trunks facing the inside of the circle. Each family is responsible for decorating their trunk (or cargo area of their SUV). Families can create scenes or carnival type activities, which can be as simple as having children stand six feet away from the trunk and tossing in orange sponges to earn a prize. Some families decorate trunks with battery operated lights and "cobwebs." Children have to reach through a plastic spiderweb to get their candy from inside the trunk.

Cleaning up is easy. Just close the trunk, get in the car, and drive home! Children enjoy getting candy and prizes in a controlled environment. Parents enjoy not having to donate hours of time constructing carnival booths.

Fun with
Home
Decorations

287. Glow-in-the-Dark Tablecloth

Supplies: old, solid-colored sheet,
fluorescent paint, paint brushes

One of the keys to successful parenting is taking ordinary events and "twisting" them into something special. Children delight in eating outside at night, especially with a tablecloth that mysteriously glows in the dark.

Purchase fluorescent paint at a craft or hobby store. (The paint costs about the same as regular acrylic paint, but produces more "ooohs" and "ahhhhs.") Go outside and set out an old solid-colored sheet to use as a tablecloth. Ask your children to decorate the sheet with the fluorescent paint. Stars, dinosaurs, self-portraits...anything goes. When the artists are done, let the paint dry thoroughly in the sun.

To make the biggest impact, remove the sheet after the paint has dried so your children don't see it. When it gets dark, dim the house lights and take the family outside for an outdoor snack. With a great flourish, spread the newly painted tablecloth on a picnic table. Watch your children's faces as they see their artwork glow in the darkness. Enjoy a snack while commenting on the eerie designs glowing up from the tablecloth. Some families use their glow-in-the-dark tablecloth inside as they turn off the lights and eat dinner by the light of a single candle.

Fun with Home Decorations

288. Special Occasion Tablecloth

Supplies: washable, light-colored plain tablecloth; permanent markers; fabric paint; newspaper

Martha Stewart may cover her dining table with an antique imported linen tablecloth made by nuns in Ireland. Your family, however, will get more pleasure out of turning an ordinary tablecloth into a treasured keepsake using fabric paint.

Purchase a washable, light-colored tablecloth. Begin a family tradition of using the tablecloth on birthdays, holidays, and anniversaries. Each time the family celebrates a special occasion, record the event on the tablecloth by asking each person to write a message, along with the date. Use permanent markers or fabric paint to write, "Best wishes on your sixteenth birthday, Jessica!" or, "Here's to another twenty-five years of a great marriage!" To prevent the colors from bleeding through to your table, slip newspaper underneath the tablecloth when people are decorating it.

Let your children sketch a picture or trace around their hands. You'll have a pictorial record of their growth as the tiny handprints get bigger each year. If using fabric paint, be sure to let the paint set completely before washing or storing the tablecloth. One family had a very ambitious grandmother who would embroider over each greeting or picture, creating a long-lasting family heirloom.

289. Creative Centerpieces

Supplies: assorted household items

Anyone watching Martha Stewart create a table center-piece on TV is amazed at her attention to detail. First she covers the table with an antique, hand-woven tablecloth. Roses, lovingly grown by nuns in a French convent, nestle picture perfect in a hand-blown vase.

Don't despair if your table sits adorned with crayon-covered plastic placemats. Instead of hiring those French nuns to raise roses for you, enlist children's help in creating practical, creative, and kid-centered centerpieces.

Assign each child a specific week for which to supply a centerpiece reflecting their interests. You may not get an elegant floral arrangement, but you might find a great dio-rama filled with jungle plants and plastic dinosaurs on the table. One soccer star placed the soccer ball in the middle of the table surrounded by his soccer shoes and shin guards. (He did scrape off most of the mud!) Perhaps your preteen will place a jar filled with marbles or buttons on the table. Family members try to guess how many items are in the jar. Children can set up a display of teddy bears having a tea party, or a miniature town filled with toy cars. Since every-one participates, everyone gets a chance to be compli-mented on his or her centerpiece. Who knows, maybe Martha Stewart will get inspiration from your family!

290. Reusable Birthday Names

Supplies: 4" x 6" colored index cards, markers, glitter, glue, stickers, paper punch, yarn or chenille stems

Your birthday party decorating box is probably filled with banners and leftover streamers. Let children add to your collection by making their own name cards to be used whenever the decorating opportunity arises.

Give children 4" x 6" index cards, colored if possible. They need one card for every letter in their name. Set out an assortment of markers, glue, stickers, and the ever-popular glitter. They write their name, with one letter per card, and decorate each card by outlining the letter in yarn, adding glitter, etc. The more elaborate the better.

After the cards are decorated, punch holes in the two top corners of each. Lay out the cards, side by side, so the child's name is spelled correctly. Use small pieces of yarn or chenille stems to hook the cards together through the punched holes. You now have a decorative banner of each child's name.

The next time a birthday arrives, add your child's banner to the bottom of a store-bought "Happy Birthday" sign. If your child gets a great report card, make a sign reading, "Congratulations on Your Hard Work" and attach their name banner. It adds a personalized touch to words of celebration.

291. Year-Round Holiday Tree

Supplies: artificial tree, holiday decorations

Children enjoy celebrating any kind of holiday. It's exciting to open Valentine's cards or wear green on St. Patrick's Day. Then there's the fun of setting up a Christmas tree with all the lights and special decorations. But come January, the tree is soon gone. Extend the holiday season by decorating a tree all year long.

Purchase a small artificial tree. Many stores sell them for half-price at the end of December. Find a "permanent" place to display the tree, since you'll see it for a long time.

Each holiday, let children decorate the tree appropriately. They can make red paper chains for Valentine's Day. On the Fourth of July, attach small American flags to the branches. When someone's birthday arrives, stick a pointed party hat on top of the tree. Cover the tree with cotton spiderwebs for Halloween. Start decorating for obscure holidays like Smokey the Bear's Birthday on August 9. Don't forget to dress up the tree on November 18...Mickey Mouse's birthday!

Fun with Home Decorations

292. Pictorial Placemats

Supplies: manila envelope, 11" x 17"
construction paper, glue, scissors

Parents always lament how quickly children grow from toddlers to preschoolers to full-fledged children. Sometimes it's hard to remember the events of the past year. Here's an easy way to keep a pictorial record of your child's experiences.

Label a large manila envelope with each child's name. Tape the envelopes to the inside of a closet or some other place that's easily accessible. Throughout the year, collect "flat" items such as funny photographs, ticket stubs from the school play, or samples of homework that relate to each child.

When a birthday approaches, go to your child's envelope and sort through the items. Make a collage from your collection, glued onto a piece of construction paper. Label it with the year and have it professionally laminated at a quick-print center. Serve the birthday child her cake on this customized placemat that can be enjoyed all year long.

These placemats serve as a wonderful reminder of your child's growth and development. It's fun eating off placemats from several years ago and commenting on the events that took place that year.

293. Travel Memento Placemats

Supplies: 12" x 18" pieces of construction paper, travel brochures, scissors, glue, markers, contact paper

"Let's save the entrance ticket for the museum!"

"Don't throw away that brochure from the zoo. I want to keep it."

Traveling with children brings out their "hoarding" instincts. You arrive home with suitcases full of brochures and travel advertisements. Instead of tossing the crumpled papers away, use them to make a travel placemat.

Give each child a large piece of colored construction paper or poster board, about 12" x 18". Sort through all the printed material. Cut out special pictures or titles such as "Disneyland." Add a few photographs from your trip also. When you have a pile of usable material, arrange the pictures on the cardboard. Use markers to draw small sketches of mosquitoes or other reminders of the trip. Be sure to put the date in a prominent location.

When you've decided on a pleasing layout, glue down all the pictures. Cover the entire placemat with clear contact paper. Another option is to have the placemat laminated at your local printer. That way you'll have a spill-proof reminder of your family trip for years to come. Make a placemat after every trip and soon you'll have a collection of several years of happy memories.

Fun with Home Decorations

The Show Must Go On

294. A Play in a Day

Supplies: three or more children, a short play or skit, costumes, basic props

Children love performing in plays, although parents aren't too fond of driving to countless rehearsals. Here's a way for children to express their dramatic abilities without hours of preparation.

Select a short play with a variety of roles. A ten- to fifteen-minute play is ideal for this venue. Better yet, have a few budding playwrights write their own play. (Naturally they'll cast themselves in the leading role, but that's creative license!) Make copies and assign parts to children who expressed interest in participating. Give each actor his or her script one week ahead of the performance. It's their responsibility to learn lines.

Set up a stage area with a few props. If you have extra chairs, set them up for the audience. If not, tell the audience to stand, like they did in Shakespeare's day.

Allow about two and a half hours on the day of the big event. A typical schedule would be:

1:00 P.M.: Rehearse the play. Have an adult nearby to keep things moving.

2:00 P.M.: Try on costumes, fix hair, and do one more dress rehearsal.

2:45 P.M.: Proud parents and friends arrive.

3:00 P.M.: The show must go on!

3:15 P.M.: Children receive a standing ovation and glowing accolades from the critics.

Even in this short amount of time, children can perform an acceptable theatrical event. This is one play where the audience is encouraged to take flash photography.

295. In-Home Museum

Supplies: paper, markers, tables, collections of items

Children seem to amass a variety of collections ranging from smooth stones to stuffed animals. Usually these "priceless" collections end up in the bottom of a toy box. If you find yourself faced with the prospect of a rainy weekend, encourage children to set up a home-base museum displaying their treasured items. If enthusiasm is still low, offer to pay admission to visit the museum.

Begin by finding a suitable museum location. Can children take over the dining room or the garage? Discuss how museums attract customers. Perhaps children want to provide hands-on activities and various exhibits of "artifacts." One museum included a delightful display of smelly socks collected from underneath a nine-year-old's bed!

It takes just a little guidance to get Junior Curators thinking about their museum. It won't be long until hobbies are displayed and labels go up explaining the exhibits. Offer to serve refreshments at the grand opening. For even more fun, invite relatives and friends over—they'd probably be willing to pay the admission fee!

296. Share the Experiences

Supplies: vacation memorabilia, snacks

You've returned from a long-anticipated trip and had wonderful experiences. Yet often we get home and immediately start in on the routine of everyday life. It's easy to forget to reflect on what you just did. Relive your trip memories by inviting over a few friends or relatives for an evening of show-and-tell travel adventures.

Don't worry, this isn't the dreaded "Look at the hours of vacation videos I took" evening. Assign each family member one aspect of the trip to share. A young child could show the shells he found at the beach. Someone else could read a few excerpts from the travel journal. Maybe someone else models the T-shirt purchased at a tourist attraction. With different people presenting their experiences, no one in the audience becomes bored.

Invite friends who've also returned from a trip and ask their family to share also. This gives everyone a chance to practice their public speaking skills! Serve snacks that relate to the places you visited. Sharing your experiences with someone else helps lock the memories in your mind.

297. Slide Show Extravaganza

Supplies: slide projector, extension cord, slide carousel, snacks

Anyone with children older than fifteen probably took slides of their darling baby before the days of readily accessible video cameras. You remember slides, don't you? Those large pictures you used to project on the living room wall? Here's a chance to have an evening of fun while embarrassing your children.

Invite several families over, asking them to dig through the back of a closet to find ten to fifteen slides from past vacations, weddings, or naked babies on bearskin rugs. As the host, your job is to track down a slide projector and extra-long extension cord. When guests arrive, have them put their slides in the carousel for later viewing. Set up the projector outside, using your garage door or the side of your house for the screen. Kids get a kick out of seeing how the slides cover an entire garage door by simply adjusting the distance of the projector.

When it gets dark, bring out the snacks and invite everyone to sit on the ground and watch the slide extravaganza. Show a slide and let people guess whom it is. Many people bring slides of their weddings, causing bursts of giggles from their children. Have families give running commentaries about the slides they brought. Younger children will want to know why the pictures aren't moving like on TV or a video. One family sponsored a "Bore-In" slide show. Guests were told to bring ten of their most boring slides. You know, those great shots of the family lined up like soldiers in front of Old Faithful. As each slide appeared, the friendly crowd groaned, "That's booorrring!" A prize was given to the lucky family voted to have the most boring slide.

298. Neighborhood Art Gala

Supplies: paper and pens (or computer)
for flyers, artwork, tape or clothespins,
index cards, snacks, tables

Most children are prolific with their artistic creations, while parents search for wall space to display the masterpieces. Solve this problem by hosting a neighborhood art show for children to display and sell their artwork.

A few days before the big event, help your children design a small flyer announcing the date and time of the show. Ask each participant to attach an index card to each piece of pottery, drawing, or arts and crafts project they submit. The card should list the artist's name, age, and a brief bio. That way people looking at Michael's painting know that he's eight years old and enjoys skateboarding. Be sure to list the price also! Since most art exhibitions offer refreshments, ask each participant to bring a dozen cookies to share. All you have to supply is juice.

The day of the event, set up several tables to display bulky artwork such as sculpture. If you have a chain-link fence, use clothespins to attach the paintings to the fence. Clotheslines also work well for hanging up lightweight art projects. As children arrive, help them display their creations around the area. Soon you'll have a crowd of art lovers oohing and ahhing over the junior Picassos. If grandparents are present, you can be sure sales will happen!

The Show Must Go On

299. Spontaneous Silly Parade

Supplies: balloons, crepe paper streamers, ribbons, tape, costumes

Everyone loves watching or participating in a parade. Instead of traveling to Pasadena for the Rose Bowl parade, plan your own in the comfort of your neighborhood.

Gather together a group of children for a spur-of-the-moment parade. Encourage everyone to bring bikes, old Halloween costumes, and scooters or in-line skates. While the children gather, set out a supply of assorted decorating supplies—nothing has to be fancy. You'll be amazed at what children come up with using crepe paper, balloons, and ribbon. Half the fun is using tape to attach streamers to wagons and scooter handles. It won't take long before you have children dressed in outlandish costumes with bikes covered in colorful balloons. Don't forget to have them decorate their helmets! Adults can help younger children decorate their strollers.

When the decorating extravaganza is complete, take a ride around the block, waving to lucky observers. For a full-blown parade effect, carry a battery-operated boom box blasting out marching music. More than likely, the children will want to circle the block again, and again, and again....

If you live in a neighborhood populated with children, word of the parade will spread quickly. You'll have happy adults sitting by the sidewalks, waving to the moving spectacle. This is also a great idea for birthday parties, since it helps everyone to get rid of that birthday party energy.

300. Brown Bag Skits

Supplies: brown paper grocery bags, assorted hats, toys, household items

Summer camps use this activity year after year because it's a guaranteed winner for fun and laughter. The next time you have a large group at your house, bring out the brown bags and get ready for comedy and pathos.

Ahead of time, go through the house and collect an assortment of items ranging from dirty socks to a bunch of bananas. Divide your group into teams of three or four people. Hand each group a brown paper bag containing three of the weird items you collected earlier. Let each group take five to ten minutes to plan a skit that incorporates the items in their bag. You'll feel the energy level rising as team members debate how to put on a skit that includes a dog bowl, melted crayons, and a box of stale crackers.

After rehearsal time, let each team perform for the rest of the group. You'll be amazed at the creativity! For a slight variation on this game, give each group the same three items such as a shoe, a book, and a ball. Everyone enjoys seeing how each skit is totally different, even though they have the same items to use.

The Show Must Go On

301. Three-Ring Circus

Supplies: large flat playing area; costumes; props such as balls, brooms or wooden spoons, pillows, bucket; scrap paper; animals; animal crackers

What parent hasn't at one time or another complained, "My life is like a circus"? Instead of running away to actually join the circus, harness your children's energy and encourage their creativity by letting them form their own three-ring circus.

Try it the next time you host a party or have a group of children visiting. Children love to perform. It only takes a small amount of guidance from an adult to set the theme. And you don't have to be limited to a three-ring circus; you can have five different acts going at once! A few performances could be:

- Baton twirlers using brooms or wooden spoons
- Jugglers tossing pillows with wild abandon
- Clowns who throw buckets of "water" (actually shredded paper) onto the audience
- Wild animals (such as your dog) performing feats like "roll over," "play dead," and "speak!"
- High-flying trapeze artists performing on the backyard swing set
- Fast-footed tap dancers in last year's dance recital costumes

Set out a few costumes and props and get ready for a first-rate performance. All you have to do is arrange for an appreciative audience. Ask parents or younger siblings to sit and applaud for every act. Usually the audience will call, "Encore! Encore!" and you'll get to see the circus repeated in its entirety. Afterward, serve the talented cast juice and circus animal cookies.

About the Author

For ten years Silvana Clark was a recreation supervisor and camp program director, running family activities for groups of up to several thousand people. She is the author of *600 Tips for Early Childhood Directors*, *150 Ways to Raise Creative Confident Kids*, and *Parent Tested Ways to Grow Your Child's Confidence*. She was recognized as Outstanding Recreation Programmer for the state of Washington, and received the 1997 Directors' Choice Award from *Early Childhood* Magazine. Presently, Silvana is a professional speaker, giving workshops and keynote speeches across the country. She lives in Bellingham, WA.